This book is dedicated to my mother and father—to the self-esteem they were committed to in all of their children, to the daily, weekly, and monthly small stuff they were willing to do year after year. I finally get it.

REVOLUTION
EVENT DESIGN AND PRODUCTION
WWW.EVENTREVOLUTION.COM | 410.538.7238
2000 WASHINGTON BLVD SUITE 20108 BALTIMORE, MD
Erin Cermak: etc@eventrevolution.com

www.mascotbooks.com

For more information, please contact:
Mascot Books
620 Herndon Parkway, Suite 320
Herndon, VA 20170
info@mascotbooks.com

Change Process Diagram provided by Virginia Satir Global Network

CPSIA Code: PBANG0218A
ISBN-13: 978-1-68401-516-0
Library of Congress Control Number: 2017919445

Printed in the United States

HOW TO BE YOUR BIGGEST FAN!

Renee Cermak

THE VALUE & POWER OF HIGH SELF-ESTEEM

PREFACE

WHAT IS SELF-ESTEEM? WHY DO I HAVE TO PAY ATTENTION TO MINE?

Your level of self-esteem is the number one indicator of whether you live an extraordinary life—or not. Why? To put it simply, you bring your self-estimate to everything you do and every place you go. Your opinion of yourself touches every single aspect of your life, from your relationships to your career, and from your financial security to your physical well-being. But it doesn't just influence the "big" things in life. How you feel about yourself colors *every* experience you have, from how you interact with the barista at your local coffee shop to how you respond to small irritations like traffic gridlock. And it is reflected in every decision you make, no matter how small it may seem—fast food or healthy salad; gym workout or sleep in?

In other words, you cannot detach from your self-esteem. Throughout your life, many things are likely to change, including your career, your financial status, your lifestyle, and even the people you spend your time with. But one thing won't change; for better or worse, it's *you and your self-esteem for the rest of your life.*

After being in a career I enjoyed for a long time, I found that I was burned out and needed to take a break. I was 36 years old when I made the choice to "retire," which ended up being more complicated than I could have expected. It was during this time that some simple truths became clear: if liking yourself isn't on the top of your list, then you may be missing out on the results in life you desire and deserve. If you don't value yourself, you're not going to value your life.

You see, I gained my self-esteem (worth) from my job and when that source went away, I didn't have the daily routine anymore that contributed to my self-esteem. In retirement, it became apparent quickly that I was out of balance as far as my sources of self-esteem were concerned. Much like investing, I realized I had to diversify the sources of my self-esteem.

I began writing this book as a way to discover how to increase my own self-esteem. It quickly became clear that what I was writing could also be a resource to help guide and support others on their journey.

Self-esteem isn't something most of us think about very often. It doesn't help that self-esteem is, at best, a vague concept. If asked, most people would agree it's important, just like gravity and electricity. We know it's a good thing to have, and the more the better. We know low self-esteem produces problems. Yet beyond that, it can be difficult to define.

Perhaps the best way of thinking about self-esteem is as the sum total of all of the views and opinions you have about yourself that shape your self-belief, self-worth, self-respect, self-confidence, and how much you like yourself. The operational word here is "self," because it's not about what your family, friends, or neighbors think. It's how *you* feel about you.

Granted, this is still somewhat vague, as far as definitions go. That's because self-esteem is itself a somewhat "fuzzy" concept that doesn't have sharp and clear edges. But the fact that a concept is fuzzy doesn't mean it's not vitally important in our lives. It's almost impossible to define concepts like "love" or "generosity," too. But when we feel love—or see it in others—we know exactly what it is and how important it is to have it in our lives.

The same is true for self-esteem; we know it when we see it. It's not at all difficult to recognize people with high self-esteem by what they do, the characteristics they display, and their results. People with high self-esteem:

- Lead rather than follow.
- Attract and build relationships with other successful people.
- Ask for and get paid what they are worth.
- Save for retirement, because they value their future well-being.
- Take more risks.
- Are willing to put themselves in the spotlight and public eye.
- Take care of themselves physically with adequate exercise and a healthy diet.
- Are life-long learners, taking classes, seminars, and reading educational books.
- Listen to others, but form and state their own opinions.
- Don't assume they know everything, and ask questions to gain the knowledge or information they need.
- Give their time and money to help their communities.
- Focus on how they will rather than why they can't.
- See abundance rather than scarcity.
- Are committed to creating the end results they desire.
- Are open, honest, and authentic about who they are.
- Bring more of themselves to the party.

"For many people, much of their life is organized around the circumstances in their lives. For others, much of their lives are organized around creating what they want to create. There is a dramatic difference between the two orientations. In the first, you are always subject to the whims of circumstances. In the other, you are the predominant creative force in your own life, and circumstances are one of the forces you use in the creative process."

- ROBERT FRITZ -

The biggest outward difference between someone with high self-esteem versus someone with low self-esteem lies in *results*. People with higher self-esteem levels are more likely to have thoughts and engage in behaviors that, over time, create positive results. As you can see from the list you just read, it is these characteristics and behaviors that set them apart from others and allow them to create extraordinary lives.

For most of us, self-esteem isn't something we think about very often. Even the people who understand the importance of building a child's self-esteem may struggle with paying attention to their own. We may occasionally wish we felt more self-confident, but only in passing. We rarely think about our own self-esteem with the same sort of immediacy and urgency as we think about what to cook for dinner, how to secure good childcare, or a malfunctioning Internet connection. I'm willing to bet most people think more about what clothes they wear and their car maintenance than about their self-esteem.

Most people simply don't realize improving their self-esteem can radically improve every aspect of their lives. That's because the essence of self-esteem is liking yourself. And the more you like yourself, the better you treat not only yourself, but also all of the other parts of your life that matter to you—your family, your friends, your finances, your career, your reputation, your community, your future, and your legacy. Paying attention to, and taking good care of, all of these parts of your life will lead to better and more positive results in each. That's why self-esteem matters and why *the way you feel about you is the most important thing in the world*. Or at least, in *your* world.

CAN YOU REALLY CHANGE HOW YOU FEEL ABOUT YOURSELF?

"Your life only gets better when you get better."

- BRIAN TRACY -

You may be wondering whether someone with a lower level of self-esteem can do anything about it. That's something I hear quite frequently, and what it usually means is, "Is change *really* possible?" It's a perfectly legitimate question, and it's easy to understand where it comes from. What seems to be at its root is a certain idea, which is that by the time we are adults we are set in our ways and almost nothing can alter that. The problem is this belief is simply not true, but it certainly is powerful!

Everything is capable of change. Even those things which appear static in nature, such as rocks and mountains, change over time in response to the forces of wind, rain, and the environment.

Someone asked me, "Renee, with all of the personal growth you have experienced and the personal growth you have witnessed countless people experience, *do you really think people change?*"

Through the personal growth seminars I facilitate, I am blessed in that I get to help others shift their beliefs in a positive direction that changes their lives.

I have seen people say yes to goals they knew were extremely difficult. I have witnessed people paralyzed by fear, yet still courageously take action. They faced their challenge because what they wanted for their future was more important than being uncomfortable and inconvenienced. I have seen people take outrageous actions because of their commitment to a goal or just to prove they can.

After their accomplishment, their eyes light up in wonder when they realize their goal was not bigger than them.

I have seen people who wanted to do it their way and pick up their "toys" and leave. Then five minutes later they let go of their limiting beliefs and *need to be right* and walked back in to kick fear in the face. I have seen people experience the best parts of themselves and the worst parts of themselves—all parts. I have seen people face the parts of themselves they struggled with and still make changes to become who they wanted to be. I have witnessed people reclaim their warrior spirit.

I have watched people take a stand for what matters most to them, to love, dream, be accountable, accept responsibility, be okay with being a beginner, be self-aware, be willing to sing and dance, put on costumes, experience failure and disappointment, dust themselves off, and *get back up again.* I have seen people take their relationships to a whole new level and love deeper than they thought possible. I have watched them change from victims to creators when they realize they have full control over creating and designing a life of their dreams. I have watched people not only *like* themselves but *fall in love* with themselves.

> "Courage is not the absence of fear, but rather the judgment that something else is more important than fear."
>
> - AMBROSE REDMOON -

What I do know is that regardless of how low someone's self-esteem is, or how much of a disunity currently exists between their desires and their present life, improvement is always possible. I know it is possible for people's self-esteem levels to change, because I've

AS YOU READ THIS BOOK, you will see many teachings from "The Universe." These come from Mike Dooley at Tut.com, who distributes daily "Notes from the Universe." *Thank you to Mike Dooley at Tut.com for those notes.* These quotations have helped me articulate my thoughts more eloquently, and I know they will help you focus your thoughts, also. Frequently, thoughts rumble around in my head, and they come out in a jumbled mess. Then I get a "Note from the Universe" that describes exactly what I am thinking. The Notes are based on Universal Laws and spiritual truths. (Please understand when I use "The Universe" in this book, it is interchangeable with God, the source, Allah. I do not wish to single out anyone's spiritual direction. I do accept there is a higher power than us and that belief permeates these pages.)

seen it happen countless times before my very eyes. And I also know when their self-esteem changes, everything else changes: the people they associate with, the depth of their relationships, the foods they eat, the amount of money they make, the risks they take, and even what they do on Friday nights...everything changes. And that's why I believe—no, I know—that by investing in your own self-esteem, *you* can change too.

I am a woman on a mission when it comes to self-esteem. My mission is to get you to think about your self-esteem before anything else and more than anything else. What you will find is your self-esteem is directly affected by the little things you do (or don't do), and you have 100% control over this "small stuff!"

> "Once the mind has been stretched by a new idea,
> it will never again return to its original size."
> - OLIVER WENDELL HOLMES, JR. -

BEGIN YOUR JOURNEY

As you read the book and begin your self-esteem improvement journey, obstacles are sure to present themselves, obstacles that get in the way of working on your self-esteem, the small stuff, your goals, and your life. When this occurs, and it will, don't let it stop you. Keep moving forward. Be prepared. Be a learner. Be willing to change to have the results you say you want.

This book is for you if you want to be the best you and you're open to identifying and overcoming roadblocks that might be holding you back from the life you want. I know after you realize how to increase your self-esteem that you'll be able to acknowledge that you deserve a better life and will have the tools that allow you to look in the mirror and like yourself. If you're that person whose internal struggles are comparable to psychological cuffs that hold you back, this book will give you the insights and tools to overcome the obstacles so you can accomplish and have the life you've always wanted. Everything about you in your life and how you live it is a direct reflection of your self-esteem, from the little stuff, like the clothes you wear and the food you eat, to the bigger stuff, like the company you work for and who you marry.

In this book, you will get:

- A unique self-esteem quiz that gives you a starting point for assessing and improving your current self-estimate (how much you like yourself).

- A series of exercises that help you build up, not chip away at, your self-esteem. To get the most out of this book, be sure to complete all of the exercises as you go.

- The *Cermak 1,000 Box Strategy*™, which is the culmination of all the other exercises in the book. It will challenge you to take on yourself and accomplish actions big and small that will improve your self-esteem.

While reading and learning, pretend you are at a buffet. You are walking through the line and you grab what resonates; you leave behind what doesn't. Through it all, you will come to appreciate the importance of small actions and how they are intimately connected to your self-esteem and your results. Are you intrigued by the possibility of becoming your biggest fan? Are you ready to see what's possible when you like yourself? If you are interested in separating yourself from the masses, read on.

PART 1

"It's not what's happening around you that determines your health, finances, or hotness, but what's happening inside of you—exclusively. You hottie."

CHAPTER 1

SELF-ESTEEM: 100% IN YOUR CONTROL

> "I would rather have the whole world against me than me against me."
>
> - DR. JOHN DEMARTINI -

How is your self-esteem? What do you think about yourself? Do you like yourself? Are you your biggest fan or your worst critic?

How do you feel about your life right now? Where are you versus where you should be? Are you happy and fulfilled or filled with regrets?

How do you view your future? Is your view optimistic, do you see your life as full of opportunities, or have you already peaked?

Can you say with confidence how much you know about your self-esteem? Is it low? Is it high? Perhaps you haven't really tried to measure it. That's OK, most people haven't given it much thought.

What if you could measure it accurately? What gets measured can be improved, so if you can pinpoint your level of self-esteem, you can then work on ways to build it so you can become your biggest fan.

Imagine you can measure your self-esteem on a meter, much like on a speedometer or fuel gauge. The life you will live when your self-esteem is in the 30s on the meter will be very different than the life you will live if your self-esteem is in the 80s. Where the needle is pointing to on the meter will dictate what kind of life you're living. One thing I can say with certainty is the higher your level of self-esteem, the more fun, fabulous, and fulfilling your life will be.

When I started working on my self-esteem, the needle on my self-esteem meter was stuck in the 20s. My results at that time reflected the fact that I had low self-esteem. I may have been full of potential, but I was not living up to it. The truth was, at 27 years old, I had already become a victim. Life had *happened* to me, life *owed* me. I did a lot of finger pointing. *It's his fault I am unhappy. It's my boss's fault that I don't have time off when I need it.* If you would have asked me if I was a victim, I would have said no. If you would have asked me if I had low self-esteem, I would have said no. If you would have asked me if I was unhappy, of course I would have said no. Clearly, the 27-year-old version of me was a bit out of touch.

This book passed through many, many versions before it arrived at its best version, yet they were all versions of the same book. Would you want to read the first version or the best version? Have you thought about the fact that there are different versions of you? There is the "40 on the self-esteem meter" version of you and the "80 on the self-esteem meter" version of you. If given a choice, which version of you would you like to experience? Bringing out the best version of you is a result of increasing your score on the self-esteem meter.

I have spent the last 19 years increasing my self-esteem—without even realizing what I was doing—by experiencing, achieving, creating, practicing, and failing. Mostly, though, by failing. I failed at dating, dieting, public speaking, parenting, coaching, rock climbing, yoga, facilitating, paddle boarding, writing a book, and achieving goals, to name a few.

I have also been willing to practice in all of these areas, which has led to success in all of them as well. Through the failure and the practice, I became better, my achievements became bigger and better, my goals became riskier, and my results grew.

And through it all, I increased my level of respect for myself, my respect for the failures and struggles I have been willing to experience, and my respect for the results I created. Through the experiences, struggles, and achievements, I was able to see the great parts of me and the not-so-great parts; both insights were very valuable.

I became very curious about myself, my beliefs, and what made me tick. *Why do I do the things I do? Why do I react when someone questions me? Why is it hard for me to receive feedback? Why do I get along with this person and not another person? Why did I get so angry with my daughter? Why did I say yes to doing that favor? Why was this goal so easy to achieve, and that other one so difficult? Why did I need to make my husband wrong?*

I was also willing to look at me, my beliefs, my habits, and my results from many different angles and perspectives. I learned that knowing as much as possible about myself was a worthy investment of time, energy, and money. I made some changes, and along the way, I found that when I am growing, experiencing, failing, and practicing, it is easy for me to like myself.

I'm committed every year to bringing a bigger, better version of myself. My current results reflect a self-esteem that is in the 80s on my meter. Not only am I winning big compared to when I first started this journey, but my family and my community are winning big, too.

My life and results are very different than when I started. I am closer to my full potential than I was 19 years ago. I am in a phenomenal marriage and my husband and I have a beautiful daughter. We have a high net worth and are giving back to our community ten-fold what I could ever have hoped to give when I was a victim. Because I value my life so much more now, I eat well and exercise often. I have a purposeful career facilitating seminars, speaking on various topics, and positively interfering in people's lives to help them change for the better. My friendships are deep and meaningful. I am constantly working on my self-esteem.

Maybe your full potential is to be President of the United States someday. Maybe your full potential is to minister the Gospel. Maybe it is to be a great parent. Living with the needle at 100 on your self-esteem meter is experiencing your full potential. With a higher self-esteem, you are able to create more of what you came here to create. Your full potential—your living from 100—will look very different from mine, and that is the most exciting part of the journey you are just now beginning: you get to decide what your results look like when you're a red-hot 100 on the self-esteem meter.

SELF-ESTEEM: A WORTHWHILE INVESTMENT

How you feel about you is the most important thing in the world.

Many people make the mistake of basing their self-worth on other people's opinions of them. What are other people going to think?

What does my friend think of me? What do my parents think of me? It is impossible to feel better about yourself if you hinge your sense of self on people and circumstances outside of yourself.

The only opinion about you that matters is yours.

Why? You bring your self-estimate to everything you do and everywhere you go. You bring your opinion of yourself to every relationship, every job, career, or moneymaking opportunity, to every exercise class, and even to every vacation. You cannot detach from your self-esteem, no matter how much you'd like to at times. It is the #1 driver, the #1 reason, for all of your results.

Your current physical health is a direct result of your self-esteem.

Your current financial position is a direct result of your self-esteem.

Your current relationships and the depth of those relationships are a direct result of your self-esteem.

Your current impact in the community is a direct result of your self-esteem.

You owe it to yourself to make your self-esteem your #1 priority— to make liking yourself a priority. *It's you and your self-esteem for the rest of your life.* Would you agree you are going to judge you for the rest of your life? And judge harshly?

Would you ever let anyone talk to you the way you talk to yourself?

What if you gave yourself someone to *like*? Someone to be *proud* of? What if you were your *biggest fan?* What if you did things to judge yourself *positively?* You can have that and more. And it won't cost you much...just a willingness to invest in you. A willingness to invest in your self-esteem.

How you feel about yourself is 100% within your control. If you acknowledge that, wouldn't that change where you put your time, energy, and focus?

There are beliefs you have about yourself and actions you take that *increase* your self-esteem. I refer to these as *self-esteem boosters*. These are best described as moments that give you pride, fill you with satisfaction, and make you smile.

There are beliefs you have about yourself and actions you take that *decrease* your self-esteem. I refer to these as *self-esteem chippers*. These are moments you feel shame or guilt. They cause you to beat yourself up or feel embarrassed by your choices. These chip away at your self-esteem like a pick-axe, diminishing its size and strength and, consequently, making it more difficult for you to reach your goals. This isn't complicated. What if you simply identified and increased your self-esteem boosters? What if you identified and decreased your self-esteem chippers?

Are you unhappy with the current results in your life? Do you blame others or make excuses? Do you point the finger at others when things aren't going your way?

Stop blaming other people and things. The responsibility for happiness and success, for high self-esteem, is your job, *solely yours*. The sooner you accept this fact, the sooner you can change your life. Once you take full responsibility for every part of your life, everything will change for you. Your ways of thinking/beliefs, actions/behaviors/habits, and your results will all change.

SCREAMING FOR SOMETHING DIFFERENT

When I was 22 years old, I was living the dream and had all the answers. I thought I was brilliant because I had just graduated from college. I thought I was invincible because I had just returned from a solo six-month trip to Europe. And I believed I was special because I lived on St. John in the U.S. Virgin Islands. I was going to the beach, scuba diving, island hopping; I had zero responsibilities. It seemed the future would be full of limitless opportunities and possibilities. One of those opportunities came from Hurricane Marilyn and her destruction. The whole island was badly damaged, so I left for three months. Last minute, I joined my best friends from high school for a month in Europe.

One of those friends had just come back from a seven-day personal growth seminar conducted on a ranch. She had a lot to say about it. She used unfamiliar seminar jargon to share her experience and in her repeated attempts to get us interested. Needless to say, we rolled our eyes, made sarcastic comments, and acted like know-it-all 23-year-olds. There was not a chance of me going to such a seminar.

Four years later, I was living in San Diego, no longer feeling brilliant or invincible. It turns out having zero responsibility, limited funds, repetitive days, and low values, combined with too much partying and my brain going unstimulated, did not help me achieve high self-esteem. I was not doing anything to learn, or grow, or be proud of myself. I was not even close to being my biggest fan.

At 27, my results accurately reflected my self-esteem. I was making $30,000 a year as a cocktail waitress. I had a college degree I was not using and had created a life of mediocrity. I smoked, drank, and partied too much. I had superficial friendships and was disconnected from my family. My self-esteem was low.

I attracted and dated men with low self-esteem as well. Not bad men, but men who were also living a life of mediocrity, men who were also unhappy. *You are unhappy, I am unhappy, let's be unhappy together.* I did not like myself very much.

And the future did not seem to be full of limitless opportunities and possibilities anymore.

There was a big difference between my 22-year-old and my 27-year-old view of myself, the world, and my outlook for the future.

I realized I did not know it all, I did not have it all together, and I
was not as special as I thought. At age 22 in the U.S. Virgin Islands,
I considered being a waitress and my lifestyle as signs of liberty. At
age 27 in San Diego, I considered being a waitress and my lifestyle
as signs of being stuck. I was not happy where I was at 27 compared
to where I expected to be, where I thought I was supposed to be, or
where I had dreams to be. And my belief about my abilities to change
any of that was null.

Anybody relate? Many people start their 20s striving for greatness
and end their 20s settling for mediocrity or "reality."

> "Some people die at 25 and aren't buried until 75."
> - BENJAMIN FRANKLIN -

One day, one of the friends I went to Europe with called. She
said, "Do you remember that class Beth was talking about while
we traveled Europe?" I said I did. She said, "Well, I just took it last
weekend, and it is extraordinary. You have to go!" Even though I
had already waited four years since I had first heard of the class,
and even with my current mediocre results, it still took me another
couple months to go. The thought of my friend moving forward
without me was the final push.

> "There are people out there screaming for something different and
> nothing is coming out of their mouth."
> - RENEE CERMAK -

I was one of those people who desperately wanted something
different, and yet, I acted as though everything was fine. This class
would be the first time it sank in that I had 100% control and
responsibility for my thinking, choices, attitude, behaviors, actions,

results, and, most importantly, *future results.* I realized if I was responsible for my results, then I had a lot to learn about how to craft an extraordinary life.

That class triggered a series of events. I started setting goals. I began surrounding myself with different people. I started doing things differently every day. I changed everything about my life— not overnight, but moment by moment, day by day. Over time, I changed my self-esteem; I changed the results in my life from average to what I considered extraordinary at the time.

I began a quest to create my future life by *design* and *choice* versus *being a victim to circumstances.* I also began the journey of *liking* myself.

Within six months, I had completed my first triathlon, been accepted to the Southwest College of Naturopathic Medicine in Tempe, Arizona (after I was told it was not possible to do so in my time frame), reconnected with my family, and attracted different kinds of people into my inner circle. These new friends were *motivated*; they had *stuff to do.*

> "I want people in my life who are more interested in my growth than my comfort."
>
> - ERIC JOHNSON -

SELF-ESTEEM QUIZ: WHAT'S YOUR NUMBER?

As I said, gaining a deeper understanding of yourself, and assessing your current level of self-esteem, can be challenging. For that reason, I've designed a tool, the Self-Esteem Quiz, to be the first step on your journey. It is intended as a way for you to determine where the needle is pointing on your self-esteem meter.

But before you get into the quiz, I'd like to say a few words about the purpose of this tool and the best way to approach it. The goal of this exercise is to give you a clear idea of your current level of self-esteem. After all, how can you chart your progress towards a bigger, better version of yourself if you don't know where you're starting from?

I'd like to stress there is no pass or fail associated with this quiz. It's simply a tool designed to help you gather *information* about where you are right now. The inherent nature of information is that it is purely neutral, neither positive nor negative. Because it's simply a collection of facts, information in its own right is immune to any judgments. For instance, if you look at a Google map of your neighborhood, you can easily find the quickest route to the local mall. That's information. But it would make no sense at all to say, "Oh, the mall is on the corner of 1st Street and 2nd Avenue, and that's good (or bad)." The mall is just where it is. And so are you. The difference, of course, is the mall can't change location. But by using the information you collect from your self-assessment, *you can change.*

So think of this quiz as your own personal "Google map" for getting from point A to point B. Your point A will not be exactly like anyone else's, any more than it would if you and a neighbor two blocks away were both starting out for the same destination. You can only start out from where you are, not from where someone else is— or even from where you wish you were at the moment. The point here is that the goal of the quiz is simply to give you the "lay of the land" and help you chart your course.

Also, please try not to judge yourself negatively. Even if your self-esteem is at rock bottom, that's OK. In fact, it's valuable information for you to have. After all, when you're starting from the bottom of a valley, the only direction you can go is up!

When I first started on my journey, my self-esteem was at an all-time low. And I'm actually grateful it was. That probably sounds strange, but when I look back on that time now, I can't help thinking if it had been even a little bit higher, I might have convinced myself it was "too good" to be considered an issue, or at least "good enough" that I didn't need to worry too much about it. And that may have been enough to prevent me from getting serious about seeking a different way.

So if the reading on your "self-esteem meter" isn't anywhere near 100, don't worry. In fact, I consider a score of 90 to 100 to be extraordinarily rare. The true value of knowing your number is it establishes a "point A," or starting point, from which to create—and launch—a plan that will help your reading soar.

The quiz on the next few pages is intended to help you determine your current level of self-esteem by looking at the results of your life *as a whole.* That's because self-esteem, or lack of it, permeates every aspect of your life. Before you begin the quiz, choose a number between 0 and 100 you think accurately reflects your self-esteem "measurement" today, and write it down here: __40__

Now you're ready to take the quiz. Here's how it works:

Each item in the quiz contains a phrase; check the box that best corresponds to your response to each phrase. The choices are: positive, negative, or neutral. So, you are going to choose the response that best expresses whether your relationship with this "item" is influencing your self-esteem in a positive way, a negative way, or has no effect at all.

If a particular phrase doesn't apply to you (for example, it mentions children and you don't have any or it mentions a significant other and you don't have one or it mentions a gynecologist and you are male), check the neutral box. (Do your best to check either the positive or negative box; try to keep the total number of neutral checks to a maximum of 10.)

If the "item" is something you avoid doing, such as calling your mother or making your bed, check the negative box.

Don't overthink your choices. Do the quiz quickly, and go with your first reaction.

Your answers should reflect your current relationship with each phrase or item, not what you'd like it to be.

SELF-ESTEEM QUIZ

· · ·

PHRASE	POSITIVE	NEGATIVE	NEUTRAL
Paying bills on time	✓		
The condition of your desk most of the time		✓	
The amount you complain	✓		
Eating a healthy breakfast regularly	✓		
The amount of your credit card debt	✓		
The amount of water you drink daily		✓	
How often you lie, even little white lies	✓		
How often you overreact, yell, or scream	✓		
How often you are on time	✓		
How often you compliment people	✓		
The cleanliness of your car		✓	
Maintaining good personal hygiene and grooming	✓		
Up to date with yearly physical		✓	
Your credit score	✓	✗	
The amount you have in savings		✓	
Your communication with your significant other	✓		

PHRASE	POSITIVE	NEGATIVE	NEUTRAL
Waking up on time consistently	✓		
Filing your taxes on time (this includes extensions)	✓		
Weekly/monthly call to your mother and/or father			✓
Returning borrowed items on time	✓		
The condition of your yard	✓		
How often you give to your significant other	✓		
How often you are willing to be a beginner and learn new skills	✓		
Sending thank you cards, texts, or emails	✓		
Parent-teacher meeting attendance	✓		
Your integrity on tax returns		✓	
Keeping & organizing memories— photos and mementos	✓		
How often you experience physical affection with your significant other	✓		
Communicating upsets and moving on		✓	
Keeping an accurate current bank register or electronic records		✓	
The house or apartment you live in	✓		
Up to date with gynecologist	✓		
Your financial knowledge		✓	
Your criminal record	✓		
Driving and not getting lost	✓		
Flossing your teeth regularly		✓	
Your ability to apologize—often and first	✓		
Organized paperwork/filing system for financial and personal items		✓	

PHRASE	POSITIVE	NEGATIVE	NEUTRAL
The amount you try new foods and experiences		✓	
Volunteering your time	✓	✗	
How often you do what you say you are going to do	✓		
Joining clubs, groups, associations, and networking	✓		
How often you have sex or intimate moments with your significant other	✓		
Sending in paperwork on time: forms, applications, bills			
The car you drive	✓		
Your level of education		✓	
The cleanliness of your house	✓		
Completing house projects to 100%	✓		
Returning messages in a timely manner		✓	
How often you attend other people's special events	✓		
Voting politically	✓		
Your religious/spiritual practice and attendance	✓		
Your pace—urgent or lazy		✓	
Recycling trash and recycling/repurposing other items	✓		
Going to cultural events: museums, concerts, and plays		✓	
Only taking money and items that belong to you	✓		
Being faithful to your significant other	✓		
How often you invite other people over to where you live	✓		

PHRASE	POSITIVE	NEGATIVE	NEUTRAL
How you dress and present yourself	✓		
How often you see your family	✓		
Your driving record	✓		
Living beneath your means		✓	
Your ability to speak in public settings or to groups of people	✓		
Having a college degree		✓	
How often you are helpful	✓		
How often you read/listen to books	✓		
How often you make new friends	✓		
The amount of hobbies or interests you have	✓		
The amount of life insurance you have		✓	
How romantic you are with your significant other		✓	
Your ability to listen	✓		
How often you give and focus on other people	✓		
Handling problems, complaints, or challenges immediately	✓		
How often you are spontaneous		✓	
How often you give your children 100% of your attention	✓		
How often you have fun	✓		
Your awareness of current events		✓	
Making your bed daily	✓		
Your integrity with money	✓		
Your ability to make the difficult phone calls		✓	
How often you smile at people	✓		
Having nice pictures of yourself	✓		
Your physical health	✓		

PHRASE	POSITIVE	NEGATIVE	NEUTRAL
Auto, home, health insurance up to date	✓		
Participation in your children's homework	✓		
How often you keep your agreements with yourself	✓		
How often you keep your agreements with others		✓	
The amount you tithe	✓		
How often you set and achieve goals	✓		
Eating fruits and vegetables	✓		
The number of friends you have and the depth of those relationships	✓		
How often you vacation	✓		
Your relationship with your significant other	✓		
Your relationship with your children	✓		
The clothes you wear	✓		
Your weight	✓		
Your diet—the foods you eat	✓		
Your communication with your kids	✓		
The amount of time you watch TV	✓		
The amount you drink or do drugs	✓		
How often you are grateful	✓		
Doing more than your share	✓		
Having a positive attitude	✓		
Up to date with the dentist	✓		
Taking vitamins and supplements		✓	
The amount of long-term friendships		✓	
Your energy level	✓		
Being knowledgeable about something	✓		
The amount you have traveled	✓		

PHRASE	POSITIVE	NEGATIVE	NEUTRAL
The amount you talk/gossip about other people	✓		

When you are finished, add up the total number of **positive** check marks. This number is your self-esteem meter reading. **Write it here:** _82_

What was the number you chose before taking the quiz? **Write it here:** _40_

And now, the all-important question: What do you *want* your self-esteem number to be? **Write it here:** _90_

If the gap between your current reading and where you want it to be is large, don't let that discourage you in the least! Don't fall into the trap of judging yourself too harshly. Treat yourself like you would expect your best friend to treat you. What would he or she say to you right now? My guess is they would help you see things in the best possible light. And in this case, that means acknowledging that no matter where your needle falls on the meter, what you've just done is take the first step towards changing your life for the better! In my opinion, that's something worth celebrating!

Perhaps the quiz has sparked some ideas already about how you can increase your number. Perhaps you are already visualizing things you'd like your future life to include. Take a moment to think about that. What would you like to do that you are not doing today? Do you want to take an art class or dance lessons? Learn a new language? Start your own business? Let your imagination run free!

My hope is that the quiz has helped you not only see where you are at currently but has also given you some insight into where you're heading on the road to enhanced self-esteem.

HOW YOU GOT HERE

Think about the qualities of a small child: honest, adventurous, curious, loving, unconditional, creative, and willing to take risks. It doesn't matter what culture the child grows up in or what gender the child is. These qualities and characteristics are inherent to all small children.

You were once a small child with all of these inherent qualities. You came into this world with everything you needed, bringing 100% of yourself to the party—we all did. What happened to the small child? You grew up, observed things, and experienced things. Life happened. And from your life experiences and examples around you, you developed beliefs or ways of thinking.

From your beliefs and the ways you think, you create your *actions* and *behaviors*. What you do. What you say. How you act. Meet Jeremy. If he believes he is capable, can trust himself and other people, and the world is friendly, how might he act? What would his *behaviors* look like? How would he act in relationships? He might be open, honest, loving, generous, and adventurous. How would he treat his physical body? He might exercise, eat well, and dress nicely. How would he act or behave in his career? He might network, take classes, offer help, and do more than his share.

Now let's meet Frank. If he believes he is not capable, can't trust himself or other people, and the world is unfriendly, how might he act? What would his *behaviors* look like? How would he act in relationships? He might act unfriendly, distant, closed off, guarded, and jealous. What would his behaviors regarding his physical body be? He might eat poorly, not exercise, and miss important doctor appointments. What actions characterize his career? He might do the least amount, not look for opportunities. He might lie or steal.

Your beliefs *create* your actions and behaviors. Your actions and behaviors become habits and, over time, produce results—results you want and results you don't want.

If Jeremy believes he is capable and his actions and behaviors align with that, what results would he produce? Now let's consider Frank. If he believes he is not capable and his actions and behaviors align with that, what results would he produce? Can you see how different their results would be?

Here is a visual model of this process:

So where does self-esteem fit in to all of this? *All of this* is your self-esteem. The following diagram is a more accurate picture of what is really happening.

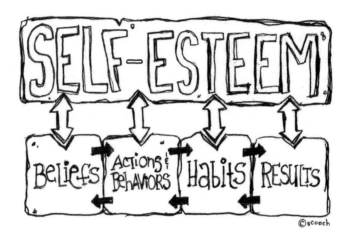

©scooch

There are many moving parts to this system. Every part of the system will affect the other parts of the system. Ultimately, this means you have choices. You can choose to change your beliefs, your actions/behaviors, your habits, your results, or your self-esteem. You can choose which area to focus on, and affect change in the other parts.

The hardest category to change is your beliefs; the easiest category to change is your habits. The way to affect the most change is by focusing on self-esteem; it affects all four categories at the same time.

I believe it could be as simple as this: If you make your self-esteem your top priority, if your purpose is to like yourself, and you focus daily on doing things that enable you to like yourself more, all of the other categories will take care of themselves. Notice I did not say if you focus daily on doing things that make you happy *in the moment.*

Taking actions to like yourself are very different than taking actions to make yourself happy in the moment. If you want to like yourself, you might eat a salad and go work out. If you want to be happy in the moment, you might eat a hamburger and take a nap.

Taking actions to simply make yourself happy in the moment will never lead you to high self-esteem.

"You can change a great many things. Or you can change. Same-Same."
- THE UNIVERSE -

YOUR DISCOVERY JOURNEY

For years now, I have strived to help people with their self-esteem through seminars and coaching. The transformation I have witnessed in thousands of people has been incredibly inspiring.

Some people are more than a little hesitant to attend a personal growth seminar where they will be compelled to spend time looking at all areas of their life and come face-to-face with what's working and what's not.

"I don't know if I want to look under those rugs," they say. "What might I find?" But after three days, 99.9% of these same people realize they are much more extraordinary than they remember. They realize, rediscover really, that they are passionate, courageous, powerful, loving, creative, supportive, and fun.

How is it they had forgotten all these wonderful things about themselves? They became adults. These qualities were still there, just forgotten, filed away. They remained unused, with baggage piled on top.

This is not true for *some* people; it is true for *all* people. When people realize they are so much more passionate, trusting, committed, courageous, powerful, loving, and fun than they think they are, they are willing to bring more of themselves to the party called *Life*. When they are willing to bring more of themselves to the party, everything changes, including their self-esteem.

This is why personal growth work—*self-esteem work*—is so vital. It is the key for you to be able to bring more, be more, and have more.

Think of this book as your personal self-esteem seminar. This book will help you rediscover that:

- You, too, have more to bring to the party.
- You, too, have forgotten how fabulous, how extraordinary, how passionate, and how fun you are.
- You are bigger than your limiting beliefs. You have control over their power.
- There might be some areas in your life where you are more committed to being right than to the end result, and you want to change this mindset.
- Being wrong about some things you have decided could be a good thing.
- You can pay prices for what you think about over and over, or you can reap rewards for what you think about. What you focus on grows.
- It's time to change the way you talk to yourself.
- Your vote is the only one that matters.
- The small stuff day after day creates every result.
- Some of your habits are not working for you.
- Excuses are just limiting beliefs in disguise.
- Your results are a matter of which beliefs you feed.
- You have the power to change the neural pathways in your brain.
- You are producing results 24 hours a day. It takes the same amount of time to produce good results as it does bad results.
- Five-year-olds have so much to teach us.
- Why it is so important to take the high road.
- Why people with high self-esteem say *no* more often than they say *yes*.

- Achieving goals is a skill. Set yourself up to win with a guide to goal achieving.

- Giving up your way is the only way to great results.

- 80% of your life is the daily grind. It's time to change your perspective.

- You are always creating your end result picture.

- Nothing is futile; everything speaks.

- When you increase your self-esteem, you increase your ability to create.

- You can be your biggest fan.

You will gain tools that will enable you to:

- Boost your self-esteem score.

- Change the small stuff you do that increases and decreases your self-esteem.

- Change your ineffective habits.

- Bring more of yourself to the party.

- Create a better reputation with *yourself* and whomever you want.

- Give up being right about your way and get more of what you want.

- Talk nicer to yourself. Change your vote about yourself.

- Make your self-esteem your #1 priority.

- Create a plan to like, respect, and be proud of yourself.

- Achieve your goals.

- How to bring more fun and passion to the not-so-great stuff.

- How to set yourself up to win through any transition.

- Create a personalized plan to increase your self-esteem.

- Use the *Cermak 1,000 Box Strategy*™ to achieve any goal you want (More about this later!).

Before we move on to the next chapter, I want to touch on one last topic. I mentioned earlier that I believe in a higher power. I believe we are each a vessel to contribute, create, or share a message. Through our self-esteem, we control how big our message is and how big the audience that receives it is. How effective we are at communicating and delivering our message depends on our self-esteem and other skills.

Imagine me communicating my message from somewhere between 10 and 50 on the self-esteem meter, basically where I am in survival mode. If I'm not meeting my basic needs, how much of my time can I spend thinking, dreaming, researching, and practicing my message? Now, imagine me communicating from an 85 on the meter.

What number will enable you to create what you came to create, communicate what you came to communicate, or to be the vessel for whatever change you are committed to? I believe your higher power wants you to be the best version of yourself for whatever you came here to do.

Imagine two people with the same innate gifts and the same message to give the world. One can choose to live life at a 25 on the self-esteem meter and be a victim of people, events, and opportunities; the other can choose to live life at an 80 on the self-esteem meter and be the predominant creator of his/her message and vessel.

Self-esteem is vital to living an exceptional life. Consider your responses on the Self-Esteem Quiz. *Is your self-esteem where you want it to be?* If not, it's likely due to your beliefs, habits, and results. Let's focus on what each of those concepts are one at a time, where they come from, how they influence self-esteem, and how you can change all of them to improve your self-esteem. First, we will look at beliefs, how your belief systems were formed, and what you can do about them now. As you'll see in the next chapter, what you believe—or don't believe—about yourself can have an enormous impact on your self-estimate, and on how much you like yourself.

CHAPTER 2

SELF-ESTEEM AND YOUR BELIEF SYSTEM

"Your mind is a garden. Your thoughts are the seeds.
You can grow flowers. Or you can grow weeds."

- RITU GHATOUREY -

THE NATURE OF BELIEFS

"What do you believe?"

"What is your belief system?"

People usually interpret questions like these as being about the *big* stuff (God, religion, spirituality, the meaning of life, morality). But we also have strong beliefs about other things that are important to us, such as how to parent, how to be in relationships, the value of money, the meaning of success, the importance of family, and on and on. We have beliefs about ourselves that are deeply personal: our value as human beings; our talents, failings, and potential; whether we are loveable or not. It's not very difficult to see how beliefs such as these can influence our self-esteem, for better or worse.

But when I talk about the connection between your beliefs and your self-esteem, I mean something much broader than these interpretations. The truth is, you have beliefs about literally everything. And when I say "everything," I really do mean everything, including thousands and thousands of "small stuff" beliefs, such as beliefs about toilet paper (over the top or under), sandwiches (crust on or off), and how beer should be poured (foam or no foam). Now at this point you may be wondering whether you really do have a belief about something as seemingly mundane as toilet paper. You may say, "I don't really care whether it rolls over or under! How is that a belief?" But if you think about it for a minute, you'll see that not really caring about toilet paper either way *is* actually based on a belief—toilet paper is too insignificant to think about.

Why does any of this matter? It matters because your beliefs, both large and small, have enormous power over every aspect of your life. And the reason that is so is that they represent your truth. In other words, if you believe something you must also accept it as true. Not a preference, not an opinion, but a factual truth. (If you have any doubts about that, try to make yourself believe something that you *know* isn't true, and you'll see what I mean.)

Your beliefs—your truths—form the foundation of the rules that you put in place to run your life and the rules you measure yourself against to assess your success. If you have a belief that being successful means earning $100,000 a year, then the "rule" you are most likely to adopt is, "I have to work hard at my career." Deciding to stay home with your infant child may then cause you a great deal of internal conflict because it means breaking your rule. Of course, if you created the rule, you can always change it to, "I am successful when I am a good parent to my child and help create a happy family life." That will change everything. But in order to be able to do that, you first need to identify the beliefs that are limiting you or holding you back.

For now, let's have a closer look at how you form your beliefs, and how they have an impact on your self-esteem.

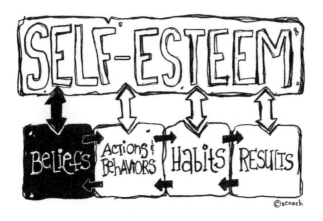

WHERE DO BELIEFS COME FROM?

In a very real sense, we "inherit" our beliefs from our parents and community as we grow up. All children come into the world with some wonderful qualities. They are honest, adventurous, curious, loving, unconditional, creative, and observant. But what they do not have is the ability to formulate their own beliefs. This is not solely— or even mostly—because of their lack of experience of the world. Rather, it has to do with their development.

> Our subconscious minds were not designed by us but by all those around
> us while we were growing up. Babies are like sponges with, literally, pure
> subconscious minds. The conscious mind (ego) has not formed yet and they
> are totally accepting of what they perceive and are told. Santa Claus is
> definitely accepted if children are told he exists. There is no judgment
> of the information.
>
> - JOHN MIKE, MD -

As life happens all around them, young children soak everything in, observing, listening, experiencing, and learning. In fact, *we acquire the majority of our beliefs by age nine,* even though we are not consciously doing so and later won't remember the process. My own five-year-old, who is constantly watching, already believes that coffee is very important (although she's never tasted it), that going to Costco with daddy means getting a present, and what being treated fairly should look like. She believes that the purse of any woman passing by is a likely source of gum or lipstick, and perhaps both. And she's already developed a system to determine which of her classmates is worthy of a valentine!

The process of acquiring beliefs is the same for any of us. From infancy, children absorb beliefs about trust, love, time, food, money, mom, dad, and the world. We are told things as children. We experience things as children. As we grow up, we see examples all around us of how to eat, how to dress, how to get along, how to handle problems, how to celebrate, how to take revenge, how to spend money, how to love, how to stay safe. And, since these examples are from people we trust and look up to, we accept them without question and later adopt them as the rules to follow in our adult lives.

By the time we become adults, we have learned that the rules matter. Or more to the point, we've learned what happens when we follow the rules and when we don't. We learn what happens when we fit in and when we don't. We learn about boundaries, punishment, rewards, risk, disappointment, loss, guilt, courage, competition, practice, society, comparing, and failure. We learn "the way that it is." We learn "the way that they are." We learn to judge ourselves, other people, experiences—everything—as either good or bad, right or wrong.

In other words, we spend the first 18 or so years of our lives attempting to make sense of the world and formulate a belief system to live by. By the time we reach adulthood, we're just a huge collection of habits and beliefs mostly learned from other people. Then we take that inherited belief system into the world as we go out on our own. That collection of beliefs determines our operating system—our actions and behaviors, for better or worse, until we critically examine these beliefs. For many, that never happens.

Most adults don't give their belief/operating system much thought, which means that they are effectively operating on autopilot most of the time. They simply follow the rules they've always followed, doing it "that way" because that's what they've always done. They don't think about whether their system is effective, because they simply don't realize that they can change their beliefs. In other words, they don't realize that their system is not everyone's system, which keeps them from seeing that there are other possible perspectives.

The problem with that is that your belief/operating system creates your reality. Regardless of the kind of childhood you had, your overall belief system will inevitably include both positive beliefs and negative beliefs based on something other than reality. Let's face it, human judgment is often prone to error. Sometimes your erroneous beliefs are inherited from others and reflect their judgment rather than your own. In other cases your beliefs may be based on an inaccuracy in how you interpret an experience, event, or conversation.

My childhood interpretation of one such event with my dad had a profound effect on me. First, let me say that my dad was one of the greats. His best attributes were his strong work ethic, his commitment to his values, his strong sense of self, his unique intelligence, and his ability to not care what other people thought. He gave me an example of how to successfully raise a large family, save and invest money, work hard and be smart—no complaints here. Sadly, he died when I was 22.

He was also extremely frugal, which meant that he always insisted on doing repairs around the house himself. Dishwasher, washing machine, car, it didn't matter. If it broke down, my dad would fix it. Of course, one of us six kids would always be called upon as his "assistant." That's why one evening around midnight, I found my 10-year-old self out in the garage holding the flashlight for him. When he asked me to hand him a tool, and I gave him the wrong one, he said, "What? Are you stupid?" And as quickly as that, a belief was formed. I immediately decided that, yes, I am stupid.

Now, don't get me wrong, my father was not in the habit of calling me stupid. It was a chance remark born, as I can now see, out of pure frustration and tiredness. And yet, it stayed with me long after many of his positive words of praise were long forgotten. In my child's mind, I interpreted the remark as applying not only to the present situation but also to every other moment for the rest of my life. It impacted my self-esteem deeply. So much so that I suspect that many of the countless things I've done over the intervening years have been unconscious attempts to gain his approval and prove my intelligence. All because of my own inaccurate interpretation of the situation!

Clearly, in spite of the fact that all of this happened at the subconscious level, my misinterpretation took a huge toll on my self-esteem. It basically integrated itself quite seamlessly into my belief system.

As I said earlier, my father is one of my heroes. I have so many great qualities because of him. I do not blame him for my belief that I am stupid. I don't blame myself either; I was 10. I made numerous inaccurate interpretations at that age—and so did you.

Unfortunately, sometimes these beliefs are decided for us and hammered into us as children. Recently, while on vacation in Mexico, we were enjoying ourselves in the pool one day. A little girl named Ellie was drawn to our many pool toys, especially our daughter's *Frozen* pool figurines. Soon Ellie was part of our group and spent most of the day with us. Her family kept an eye on her.

Ellie was well-mannered and delightful. At one point, however, her mother came over and told her, "Don't be annoying." The mother then turned to me and said, "She does not stop talking; she can be very annoying." Later, her grandfather came in the pool and pretty much said the same thing in front of Ellie. Ouch! I wondered how many hits on Ellie's self-esteem it would take before she agreed with them and stopped offering her thoughts and adopted the beliefs: *I am annoying. What I have to say isn't valuable.*

The impact of critical remarks directed at a child can be much deeper and have much more negative implications, of course, if they are repeated constantly. John Mike observes that if they are repeated often enough "messages and associated feelings like 'you are bad,' 'you can't do that,' 'that is impossible,' 'you are stupid,' all become implanted in body feelings and the subconscious mind." That is because the child's "subconscious image of who they are and what life is about is being formed not by them but by those influences around them." And although these messages are operating at the level of the subconscious mind, they impact the child's sense of self, and self-esteem, in damaging ways. And as we will see in a later chapter, when we take up the chant and repeat these same sorts of messages to ourselves, our self-esteem is wounded again, this time by our own hand.

No matter what kind of childhood you had, when you became an adult you came equipped with a belief/operating system full of limiting beliefs and inaccuracies. There is no way around it.

IF I DIDN'T CREATE MY BELIEFS, HOW CAN I BE RESPONSIBLE FOR THEM?

One of the challenges when it comes to exploring how your beliefs may be impacting your self-esteem is that they often are not only formed subconsciously, but they exert their influence in subtle, subconscious ways. This raises a bit of an apparent paradox for some people, especially in light of what I said earlier with respect to taking the uncommon path, which includes taking full responsibility for your life. The difficulty may be phrased as: "You talk about taking responsibility for my own thoughts and beliefs. But if my belief system started to form in infancy, how can that be *my* responsibility? At that stage I was just like a big sponge, soaking up what I heard, saw, and experienced, and in that sense the beliefs I hold now are really just those I was given by others. How can I take responsibility for something I didn't have any say over and wasn't even involved in creating?"

The point here is not that you are responsible for creating your own beliefs. It's that you are responsible for the beliefs *you now hold*. This does not mean, of course, that you need to—or should— simply reject all of your beliefs because they were inherited from others and start over with a clean slate. That would actually be virtually impossible because human beings simply cannot function without a belief system, especially one as broadly defined as I've been describing. It does mean that in order to live an uncommon life, it is important to take responsibility for identifying which of your beliefs are useful and worth retaining and which are limiting you and would be better replaced by more positive ones. In order to do that, of course, it is necessary to know what you believe.

> "There is an expiry date on blaming your parents for steering you in the wrong direction; the moment you are old enough to take the wheel, responsibility lies with you."
>
> - JK ROWLING -

IS A NINE-YEAR-OLD RUNNING YOUR LIFE?

The majority of what you believe today was decided by the time you were nine years old. The nine-year-old you decided something about you and relationships, money, giving, trusting, food, and everything else. What if you are able to uncover and discover the origins of your belief system, which led you to an understanding of the operating system the nine-year-old in you established? *You have the opportunity to forge a new belief/operating system that works for the life you want to create.* Who is better equipped to decide what you want to believe: *the current you or the nine-year-old you?*

As human beings, we are very committed to being right about our beliefs and view of the world. We spend our entire lives attracting people and experiences to be right about our perspective. Yet the truth is that *none of us are right.* Every one of us has a different view of the world, a different perspective on the way things are and, hence, different realities. We fight to be right about those realities and yet none of us are right.

> "Within this subconscious realm is a belief system of how we deserve to be treated and what life is about. The image we have in our subconscious minds will motivate and guide our conscious choices to fulfill that image."
>
> - JOHN MIKE, MD -

You may have an *unconscious belief* that, in order for you to win, somebody else has to lose. You may have a belief that it is okay to lose, as long as you don't lose as bad as the other guy. Or you may have a belief that there is enough for everyone to win.

You have beliefs about people and what it means to be a nice person, a rich person, a poor person, and so on. You may have a belief that you are too short, too tall, too uneducated, too educated, too young, or too old. Your current view of the world and yourself all boils down to what you have decided to believe.

Have you ever believed you were too young to achieve something, right up until the point that you believed you were too old to achieve it? According to your brain, you were either too young or too old— no age fit. But it had nothing to do with age. Whatever you thought about doing did not fit your beliefs about yourself, so you made up the beliefs that *I am too young* or *I am too old* to excuse yourself. What else are you making up?

> "Whether you think you can or think you can't, you are right."
>
> - HENRY FORD -

What might a nine-year-old have decided?

- I am not capable   or   I am capable.
- I cannot trust men/women   or   I can trust men/women.
- There is not enough   or   there is enough for all.
- I am not smart enough   or   I am smart.
- The world is mean   or   the world is friendly.
- Eat when I feel bad   or   eat when I am hungry.

LIMITING BELIEFS

No matter what kind of childhood you had, when you became an adult you had a built-in operating system full of limiting beliefs and inaccuracies. There is no way around it. *It's just the way it is. What are you going to do about it now?*

What exactly are limiting beliefs? A limiting belief is a negative, repetitive thought that you think over and over again. Limiting beliefs create false boundaries in your thinking. Your limiting beliefs show up in your reasons, justifications, and excuses. Take a moment to think of one thing that you currently want but don't have: the latest technology, a fulfilling relationship, perhaps a trip to Europe.

Now, take a moment to write down the top five reasons why you don't have that item. Maybe you are too old or too young or not skilled enough or you have kids or you don't have the time or there are not enough good men. Now, take a moment to come up with a second item that you currently want and don't have. Write down the top five reasons why you do not have this second item. Repeat the process for the third, fourth, and fifth items.

1. I want but don't have: _____

Top 5 reasons I don't have this: _____

_____

_____

_____

_____

_____

2. I want but don't have: _____

Top 5 reasons I don't have this: _____

_____

_____

_____

_____

3. I want but don't have: _____

Top 5 reasons I don't have this: _____

_____

_____

_____

_____

4. I want but don't have: _____

Top 5 reasons I don't have this: _____

_____

_____

_____

_____

5. I want but don't have: _____

Top 5 reasons I don't have this: _____

_____

_____

_____

_____

You now have a list of 25 reasons why you don't have five things you currently want. This list should give you a pretty good idea what your limiting beliefs are. You probably noticed some repetition or similarities among the lists. Whatever you allow to stop, limit, or be bigger than you in one area, you also allow to stop you in all areas. Let me let you in on a little secret...**none of your reasons or limiting beliefs are true—you made them up.** Or somebody else made them up for you and you acquiesced to them. Regardless, somehow you adopted these limiting beliefs as truth along the way.

Imagine little five-year-old Charlie trucking along, bringing 100% of himself to life and then, one day, his father leaves the family. Charlie decides that it hurts when he brings 100%, and he is going to be a little more guarded so this doesn't happen again. He also decides that he must be unlovable. Now he is going to bring only 95% of himself.

When Charlie is nine, he has his heart broken by Darlene. Charlie decides that it hurts when he brings 95% and he is going to be a little more guarded so this doesn't happen again. He also decides that girls cause pain. So, he is now going to bring 91%. When Charlie is 11, he gets beat up repeatedly by bullies and then made fun of in school. Charlie decides that it hurts when he brings 91% and he is going to be a little more guarded so this doesn't happen again.

He also decides that, clearly, he is not *enough*: not cool enough, not popular enough, not strong enough. So, he is now going to bring only 84%. When Charlie is 14, he has a misunderstanding with Heather that brings him down to 82%. When Charlie is 17, he drops the winning catch for the championship game. Charlie decides it hurts when people have such high expectations. He also learns it's better to play small. This is devastating, and so now he is going to bring only 72% of himself.

All of this happens before he is 18 years old. The sad part is that Charlie will probably only bring 72% of himself to the party for the rest of his life: his marriage, job, business, friends, kids, and hobbies. His entire life will be defined by his limiting beliefs.

And he now has four big limiting beliefs to guide him.

- I am unlovable.
- Girls cause pain; stay guarded.
- I am not enough.
- It's safer to play small.

So, this is Charlie's perspective on life. Now he will attract people and situations that confirm he is right about all of this. You can almost play out his future results. He is definitely going to have some challenges in creating great relationships.

People don't realize that what they've decided about themselves in their childhood will continue to influence and dictate future events and experiences. The nine-year-old decided that girls cause pain, and his 50-year-old self is still sabotaging relationships. The six-year-old, whose father left, decided she is unlovable, and her 40-year-old self is still attracting abusive men. The seven-year-old, whose parents fought over money, decided that money is bad, and his 30-year-old self is broke.

This may sound oversimplified, but look at your life, what you believe, how you behave, and the results you have. You are not nine, but your brain may be operating as if you are.

You may not believe it, but these limiting beliefs were created for your survival. The good news is you survived; you made it!

The bad news is they are here to make sure you *only* survive. The limiting beliefs that helped you survive are the same ones limiting you today.

There is a story about a man who, as he was passing some

elephants, suddenly stopped, confused by the fact that these huge creatures were being held by only a small rope tied from a wooden stake to their front leg. No chains, no cages. It was obvious that the elephants could, at any time, break away from their bonds, but for some reason, they did not.

He approached a nearby trainer and asked why these animals just stood there and made no attempt to get away. "Well," the trainer said, "when they were very young and much smaller, we used the same size rope to tie them. At that age, it was enough to hold them. As they grew up, they were conditioned to believe they could not break away. They believed the rope could still hold them, so they never try to break free."

The man was amazed. These animals could at any time break free from their bonds but because they believed they couldn't, they were stuck right where they were.

So, what about you? When did you start holding back? Think of a moment in your life where you know you decided to stop bringing 100%. Of course, we all have great reasons as to why we are bringing 81% or 57% or 68%. These things happened.

Now what? Are you really going to let Darlene be the reason you don't have extraordinary relationships? Are you going to let your parents be the reason you struggle with money? Don't you think you know more *now* about you, others, and the world as a 20, 30, 40, or 50-year-old? Don't you think that you are more effective at constructing a belief system than your nine-year-old self? Kids are great sponges, but they aren't prepared to equip the adult version of themselves for the rest of their lives.

If you were to design your beliefs for maximum success, to create a life that you want, what would they be?

- I can do anything.
- Making money is easy.

- I am great in relationships.
- I deserve to be happy.

Are you ready to stop being right about what the nine-year-old you decided? If you would like to know what the nine-year-old you decided, if you would like to know what you believe, just look around at your results. Look at your physical health, your clothes, your relationships, your bank account, your paycheck, and your contribution.

Ask yourself, "What am I being right about?"

What if you are not right about what you decided about yourself and money? What if you are not right about what you decided about yourself and relationships? What if you are not right about what you decided about people, men, women, lawyers, and other cultures? What if you are not right about your perspective?

"People believe what they want to believe. And this, alone, explains what they have or don't have. Does that make your entire flippin' day, or what?!"

- THE UNIVERSE -

WHAT ARE YOU WILLING TO BE WRONG ABOUT?

When I was 27 years old, my poor results fit my beliefs about me. My low income fit my beliefs about me and money. Not being in a great relationship fit my beliefs about me and relationships. So, in order for me to make a high income, I had to change my beliefs about me and money. In order for me to be in an extraordinary marriage, I had to change my beliefs about me and relationships.

At that time, I wanted to be in a great relationship, even though I wouldn't have admitted it back then. What I said instead was, "I love being single. It's more fun, less hassle. Look at those miserable married people!" Yet, that was not true.

I didn't love being single. *I was justifying my current results.* Have you ever done that before? Put whipped cream all over something you didn't like in order to justify your current results? It's pointless. But it did help me feel better, or at least made me think I felt better.

What I used to think was, "I am not good in relationships. I am not able to compromise or commit. In fact, based on my track record, I downright stink." What I really *believed* was, "Who would possibly want to be in a relationship with me?" Can you see why no extraordinary men were knocking down my door? In order to attract an extraordinary man, I had to become an extraordinary woman.

> "We don't attract what we want, but what we are."
> - JAMES ALLEN -

At 27 years old, I was not an extraordinary woman. I was a victim. I blamed other people and outside circumstances for my unhappiness. *I am grateful I did not meet my husband then. He would have kept walking.*

Today, my results still fit my beliefs about myself. However, now my beliefs are different, my thinking is much bigger, and my life and results reflect that. I honestly believe that my husband is the luckiest man in the world because he has me. That is very different from what I thought 19 years ago. Notice that the world and men didn't change, but my beliefs about myself did.

Your results today fit your beliefs about you. How do I know? Because those are your results. The amount of money you make right now fits your current beliefs about you. Making more money does not fit your current belief structure or else you *would* be making more money. It's the same for all the other areas of your life. Your results in your relationships fit your beliefs about you. Your results in your physical health fit your beliefs about you.

Results don't lie. Here is what some of those not-so-great current results might be: overweight, divorced, exhausted, overwhelmed, broke, unhappy relationship, few real friends, or feeling like you are stuck in an endless *Groundhog Day*.

The way you live your life gives you clues about your limiting beliefs. In order for you to have produced these results, what must you believe? *Which of these beliefs are you willing to be wrong about?* This is a good place to start. I am so grateful to have been wrong about many of my beliefs about me and success, money, marriage, and being a great parent.

In your introspection, you probably discovered some areas in which you are living a pretty great life. Maybe you rate your marriage a nine out of 10, you make $200,000 per year, and your children are thriving. These results give you clues about your non-limiting beliefs. In order to have produced these results, what must you believe? *Is there still room for growth?* Are you willing to be wrong about a nine to achieve a 10+ in your marriage? Are you willing to be wrong about $200,000 to make $500,000?

> "You get what you pay for and you pay for what you think about. Literally."
>
> - THE UNIVERSE -

HOW DO YOU TALK TO YOURSELF?

You spend 24 hours a day with yourself. How do you talk to yourself during those 24 hours? I imagine this extra, invisible head with a big mouth that sits on my shoulder and talks and talks all day long.

What are you saying to yourself all day long? Does that dialogue support what you say you want?

Go! Go! You are the greatest! You got this! You can do it!

Or is it self-limiting?

Who do you think you are? You are not smart/strong/valuable/good enough!

Would you ever let anyone talk to you the way you talk to yourself? *Never!* What do you say to yourself when you beat yourself up? "I am so stupid. I am an idiot. I am so bad at math. Nobody likes me." Or worse! Every time you talk to yourself that way, you are chipping away at your self-esteem. How you talk to yourself on a daily basis is a great example of small daily actions, repeated, that can lead to building up, or tearing down, your self-esteem.

If, today, Sam calls himself an idiot five times, beats himself up for his uncool clothes four times, chickens out from talking to a girl twice, then calls himself a loser 20 times, that's 31 chips in his self-esteem just *today*. This is how Sam talks to himself; these are his beliefs about himself, his *I am* statements running through his head all day long. *Like a cartoon: Thwack. Pow. Bop. Smack. Bam. Thunk.* These *I am* statements are chipping away at his self-esteem:

- I am an idiot.
- I am uncool.
- I am a coward.
- I am a loser.

How can he possibly have a high estimate of himself if this is what he tells himself all day long? How can anyone vote for you, believe in you, if you don't first have that level of faith in yourself? What if he changed the way he talked to himself? It would clear the way for him to feel good, even great, about himself—and the same for you.

Here is a story that illustrates how limiting beliefs can hurt us and how we can change those beliefs to create results:

66 Shortly after leaving my 20+ year career in property management, a coworker and I started our own business as trainers and speakers. I was always a great employee and produced amazing results. However, working for myself was a different story. Although I knew I had tons of experience and great information to share, negative thoughts would take over my brain, and all I could hear at times was, "You're not good enough; who would want to hire you? Who do you think you are?" etc. It didn't take long until we were hired for a few paid training seminars and even a couple of speaking engagements; but they were small. What I wanted was a large audience, but I also knew that my belief system about myself was not in alignment with what I wanted, and that the Universe would only deliver what I believed. I decided I had to change those negative thoughts if I ever wanted to be a public speaker. Whenever a negative thought would enter my thoughts, I would stop whatever I was doing and visualize myself on stage, speaking. My long dark hair was perfectly groomed. I was wearing a black tailored suit and a white blouse with the collar over the lapels. I was using one of those microphones that went over my ear, and I could see the audience engaged and laughing. I could also see my best friend and coworker (who lives in Portland, Oregon) in the audience. She was smiling and wearing a look of approval.

Do you see the picture? So did I, over and over again.

A couple of months later, a complete stranger from Portland, Oregon, called. She was looking for a fresh face, a new speaker with fresh information to present. She had heard great things about our coaching and consulting business. Two months later, I was on a stage in Portland, speaking to a large audience. My suit was different than I imagined, but everything else was the same, including seeing my dear friend in the audience smiling as I pursued my dreams. **99**

-Bridget Clark

This is a great example. Not only was Bridget aware of how she was feeling and her limiting beliefs, she created an action to positively interfere with the belief when it arrived.

When you become aware of negative *I am* thoughts running through your head, you can take action—do something different and positive. *Awareness is a step; action is the key.* Many people, especially in the personal growth arena, are aware of countless limitations yet do nothing about them.

Awareness does not increase self-esteem; action increases self-esteem. Results increase self-esteem. In fact, awareness without action will decrease your self-esteem. That's what happens when you don't do the things you "should" be doing, especially when you are enlightened.

Simply put, your *I am* list is running the whole show, and your *I am* list is simply your beliefs about yourself. What are your *I am* statements? Are you unique, respected, selfish, a good parent, handy, fat, lazy, stupid, smart, disciplined, a leader, a gossip, a good friend, impatient, thoughtful, happy, unfulfilled, sexy, boring, intelligent, a failure, remarkable? If you change what you say to yourself, you will change your *I am* list. If you change your *I am* list, you will change your beliefs.

I want to be clear that I am not talking about affirmations. I am talking about action. The fastest way to change what you say to yourself is to experience yourself differently by taking different and bigger actions and by producing evidence through results.

Let's say that I have *I am* statements that say, "I am lazy, not in shape, and unhealthy." If I simply stood in front of the mirror every day for a year saying the affirmations, "I am active, in shape, and healthy," how much progress would I make? Now, imagine that instead I go to the gym and work out for 45 minutes every day and *then* say my affirmations. Do you think I will be talking to myself differently after one year? How about two years? The longer I take consistent action, the bigger the difference in what I say to myself. I am not against affirmations. However, they must be used in conjunction with action.

Write down 10 of your most prevailing *I am* statements that you say to yourself on a regular basis. Think of your self-esteem score from Chapter 1 and how it connects to these beliefs.

The 10 *I am* statements I say to myself most often:

1. _____

2. _____

3. _____

4. _____

5. _____

6. _____

7. _____

8. _____

9. _____

10. _____

Think about what you would have to do to change these *I am* statements to positively impact your self-esteem score.

YOUR VOTE

Your vote about you is the only vote that matters; nobody else's vote about you matters. You may think that your significant other's, parent's or children's opinion of you is a big contributor to your self-esteem, but you spend 24 hours a day with *you*.

How much time per day do you spend with your significant other, parent, or child? Of course, their opinion of you matters to you, but they can't look in the mirror for you or shake hands for you. Your significant other cannot alter your integrity.

You are 100% responsible for who looks back at you in the mirror. Think about it: others may consider you to be a highly successful person. They may compliment you on your numerous accomplishments, viewing you as a terrific friend, parent, significant other, or employee. None of that matters, though, if you secretly believe, "If only you knew everything about me, you would not have this opinion of me." They can give you all the accolades in the world, but if the accolades don't fit your beliefs about yourself, you will internally negate every one.

For a moment, imagine how you would feel if you watched a video of yourself from the last seven days, 24 hours a day. Consider everything you did—from brushing your teeth or not, to whether or not you've followed through with your obligations, big and small. What would be on the video? Everything you did or didn't do, everything you said or didn't say, from the moment you got up to the moment you went to bed. A play-by-play of your daily actions, interactions, attitudes, and behaviors—all the small stuff. You would get to see your choices moment-by-moment and how they determined what you did with your 24 hours. This video would consist of all the things that nobody else knows about.

This is the reason why yours is the only vote that matters. Take a couple of minutes and play the video through your mind.

Nobody knows whether you:
- Flossed your teeth.
- Made your bed.

- Bragged too much or too little.
- Apologized first or not at all.
- Watched TV for zero or for four hours every night.
- Cleaned your bathroom or not.
- Returned the shopping cart or picked up the trash.
- Contributed money to a charity.
- Were nice to your mother.
- Rescheduled your dentist appointment (again).
- Spent money you didn't have or stayed on budget.
- Kept your paperwork organized or disorganized.
- Ate too much fast food.
- Took your vitamins, drank water, ate healthy.
- Stole from work.
- Left work 5 minutes early or came to work 5 minutes early.
- Were a good friend.
- Gossiped.
- Read the book to your child as promised or made it to her/his game.
- Spoke honestly about your financial position.
- Returned borrowed items.
- Exercised regularly.
- Babysat for a friend or helped someone move.
- Were scared and did it anyway or chickened out.
- Sat on the couch or visited a museum.
- Told a lie.

What's in your video? What did you see that you liked? What do you want to keep doing?

_____

_____

_____

What did you see that you didn't like or want to do less of?

_____

_____

_____

WOULD YOU DATE YOURSELF?

Now, ask yourself the following: *Would I date myself? Would I hire myself?* If the answer is "no" to either question, why not?

What would you need to start doing? What would you need to stop doing? What would you need to do to be datable or hirable to *you*? What do you need to do to like yourself? The next chapter focuses on the small stuff: the daily and weekly stuff and how it affects your self-esteem—all the stuff that is in your video.

Even though nobody knows if you showed up early, went to church, slept in, paid your bills on time, owe money, etc., *you* are aware of it. Remember: your vote is the one that counts! What you believe about yourself is fundamental to every result in your life! You will take this view of yourself—whether it's positive or negative—and not only base your self-esteem on it, but also project it to the world in one way or another.

You are very much like a living, breathing business, selling yourself all day long. The question is: how effectively are you selling yourself? If you wouldn't date yourself and you wouldn't hire yourself, then you're not really able to sell yourself, are you? Not surprisingly, it's going to be difficult—if not impossible—to get a better job or date a better person until your self-estimate matches the jobs, people, and situations you want to align yourself with.

When my husband was 22 years old, he was working with a mentor. His mentor asked him to make a list of the qualities of his ideal woman. His list: she has a great physical body, is smart, rich, fun, and has her own car. Granted, it is not the most enlightened "ideal woman list," but at 22, it was a start. When his mentor saw the list he said, "Now what would a woman like that want with a guy like you?" My husband wasn't any of the things on his list. In fact, at the time, he was living with his mother, driving her car, and not making very much money. And not long before that, he had been homeless and living on the streets.

He started making different choices, which created different results, which changed his beliefs about himself. Choices like working out, not drinking, joining the Army, getting his MBA, educating himself financially, and attending seminars that focused on personal improvement. With constant work, dedication, and determination, he became the man who could attract a woman with the qualities he listed and a whole lot more.

When he changed his actions and behaviors, his habits changed. When his habits changed, his self-esteem increased and he achieved better results. When his self-esteem increased, he changed his beliefs about the value of education and his capabilities. The result was an MBA. With an increased self-esteem, his beliefs about the value of money and his capabilities to make money changed. As he changed his beliefs, his actions and behaviors changed. The result is a high net worth.

All of these parts—the change in beliefs, the change in action and behaviors, and the change in results—collectively produced an increased level of self-esteem. An increased self-esteem supported a change in beliefs, a change in behavior, and bigger results. All pieces affect the other pieces.

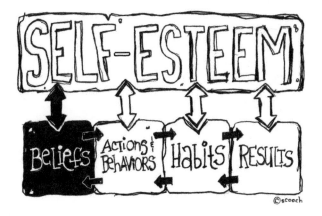

And it all starts with the beliefs. The great news is that your beliefs can be changed. However, before you look at changing anything, you have to look at the whole picture first. In the next chapter, we are going to look at the actions and behaviors that make up your habits and how those influence your self-esteem.

CHAPTER 3
EMBRACE THE SMALL STUFF

"Nobody is who they are based upon one decision, one day, one path,
one chance, one relationship, or one anything else.
Every day is brand new and opportunity never stops knocking.
Who's there?"

- THE UNIVERSE -

I am 46 years old, and I do not like the wrinkles on my face.
I notice myself comparing my wrinkles to other people's, then feeling
better or worse. I'm aware that I avoid looking at them at times.
I hear myself justifying how they got there. "I can't help it if I smile
often and my eyes like to smile too," and, "I spent a year in the
Arizona desert moving Saguaro cacti, of course I have wrinkles."

I notice myself playing up my other strengths to myself so that the
wrinkles are not so bad. "My body looks good for 46." Clearly, my
wrinkles chip away at my self-esteem. I think to myself, "How did this
happen?" And then I hear this little voice in my head say, "Really?!
Well, it certainly isn't rocket science." I can remember being 16 years
old and feeling invincible; wrinkles didn't apply to me. I remember
baking on the Maryland beaches, slathered with tanning oil.
I remember living in the U.S. Virgin Islands in my early twenties and
hardly ever using sunscreen.

I used sunscreen so I wouldn't get burned, not as a strategy
for skincare. If I were to count up how many nights I carelessly

went straight to bed without washing my face, even leaving on my makeup, I would be embarrassed. I could be honest and talk about the amount of cigarettes I have smoked or my poor diet. Because of my resistance to daily maintenance, I did not have a skincare regimen until I was 35.

My regimen goes something like this: on for 30 days, off for three months, really diligent for four days, careless for seven. And I have the nerve to ask *how did this happen?* Please! It happened from doing or not doing very small things day after day, month after month, year after year. My wrinkles did not come from one source over and over again; they came from at least 20 sources over and over again. From all of my *small actions or inactions.*

Seemingly "meaningless" decisions or moments in your life are actually very meaningful as they build and build, creating habits— habits both good and bad. These habits establish your results. Your results influence the way you view yourself. Being aware of how critical all of these small details are is one way to fundamentally shift your thinking and raise your self-esteem.

THE IMPORTANCE OF THE SMALL STUFF

> "It has long been an axiom of mine that the little things
> are infinitely the most important."
>
> - SIR ARTHUR CONAN DOYLE -

I used to think that self-esteem was built primarily from the really big moments, such as being in the school play, receiving an award, or graduating from college—the moments that are few and far between. However, as I studied self-esteem, I realized that we don't get the bulk of our self-esteem from the big moments; we get it from the small moments, the everyday moments.

I once heard a speaker say that only 10% of life is made up of the really great exciting moments, another 10% is made up of the horribly tragic moments, and 80% is what's left: everyday life, days like today. What some call the daily grind. This rang true to me.

If 80% of life is the small stuff, the daily, weekly stuff, the daily grind, then 80% of your self-esteem comes from days *just like today*. I am talking about your daily interactions with yourself, your significant other, your kids, and everybody else. Think about how you spend your money and your time. I am talking about taking your vitamins, washing your face, flossing your teeth. Look at the daily agreements you make with yourself regarding exercise, diet, finances, and the daily agreements you make with others. The majority of your self-esteem is made up of the small stuff you do every day.

- The things you do or don't do.
- The things you say or don't say.
- How you align or don't align with your values.
- The actions or inactions towards your goals.
- The agreements you make or break.

- The behaviors that you exhibit.
- The things you say to yourself.
- The little things that some say don't matter.

Your current self-esteem has been made moment by moment for at least the last 20, 30, or 40 years, like millions of grains of sand, each one seemingly insignificant, yet able to create a gigantic sand castle—or a very average mound.

Everything speaks. All the little stuff matters.

The small stuff is subtle. The small stuff doesn't produce a result the first time or the second time or the third time or the fifteenth time. Y*our self-esteem is collectively produced over time, just like the wrinkles on my face.* Whether you are overweight or physically fit, in debt or wealthy, divorced or in a great marriage—all of these results are because of the accumulation of small stuff.

The same 10,000 opportunities can produce significantly diverse outcomes, depending on your choices. Take two couples: one couple uses the 10,000 opportunities to create a phenomenal partnership, while the other couple uses 10,000 opportunities to create a divorce. It takes thousands of times to produce most results. Things don't happen overnight. The end result comes from countless combined events, not just one. Over time, the little things you do will compound.

- It takes thousands of days of not flossing for your teeth to fall out.
- It takes thousands of times of eating what you shouldn't to become overweight.
- It takes hundreds of times of working out to be muscular.
- It takes thousands of times of giving, communicating, and empowering to create a great relationship.
- It takes thousands of times of turning away, withholding,

stonewalling, and criticizing to create a divorce.

- It takes thousands of times of saving, saying no, and living beneath your means to be prepared for retirement or to build wealth.
- It takes thousands of times of spending, avoiding, and living above your means to not be prepared for retirement or to be in debt.

Certainly, some actions create a result after the first time. You can be fired after being late one time. You can acquire a bad reputation after one experience. You can find a job by sending one resume. These are the exceptions. The majority of end results are because of the small stuff, day after day.

Although it is easy to discount those 10,000 small moments and choices, they ALL add up over time, giving you your net result. In Chapter 9, you will discover the *Cermak 1,000 Box Strategy* ™ to further illuminate this idea.

Most people tend to justify the little things they do or don't do, thinking that the small stuff doesn't matter. We think things like:

- It was only one time!
- Who's going to know?
- Compared to him, I'm doing pretty well!
- It doesn't make a difference, anyway.
- Yes, I was 30 minutes late, and nobody died.
- It's not important to me.
- Everyone else does it.

While it's true that not keeping your agreement with your friend this one time may not lead to catastrophe, a *habit* of breaking your agreements will destroy any friendship. When you combine all of the little things you have or haven't done, you get measurable results—both positive and negative. These results come in a variety of forms—your reputation, your income level, your current health, and so on. When we try to justify the little things that sabotage our chances for success, we end up preventing ourselves from taking certain actions and rationalizing why we don't need to do the small stuff; but we must do the small stuff and pay attention to what we say to ourselves about it.

For example, Jack gets down on himself for having a dirty car. Every time he gets into his car, a little voice inside his head says, "Look at this car. This is a mess. Why do you do this? Blah, blah, blah." So, if Jack needs to use his car five times a day, then his self-esteem is going to take a hit five times a day—and this only includes the irritation he experiences over the car. These are not the only actions that decrease his self-esteem: Jack might also experience a chip in his self-esteem over a late fee, forgetting to call his mother on her birthday, his shirt being wrinkled, or how he treats other people. Do you see how these "small things" can add up?

Now, consider Rebecca. She really wants to exercise, but she keeps putting it off. Somewhere in the back of her mind—she's not even conscious of it all the time—she nags herself about not going to the gym or not going on that run. She says things to herself, like, "You are lazy. You are still fat. Other people who work out are better than you." This continues day after day, week after week, month after month. Think of the toll that that constant negativity takes on Rebecca's self-esteem.

Fortunately, it can work the other way, too. Let's say Rebecca begins to follow through on her daily commitment to get active. Each day that she goes for a run, lifts weights, or swims, she will become more confident and develop a positive attitude. Over time, the way she views herself will change. Instead of her old, self-defeating thoughts, she will begin to think, "I am amazing. I am healthy and active and getting better every day."

The small stuff is different for everyone. The small stuff that affects me could be very different than the small stuff that affects you. You *know* what your small stuff is. Maybe you're like Jack, the type of person who can't stand a dirty car. Or maybe you're not like Jack at all because you could care less if your car is dirty or clean. Maybe you are like Rebecca and have been putting off working on your physical fitness, and you tear down your self-esteem daily because you are not keeping your commitment.

Your first step, though, in becoming more aware of how the small stuff affects your life is to identify these ways of thinking and behaviors more specifically. Be careful in skipping over something that you think doesn't apply to you, or even skipping over something you say is not important to you.

As a coach and facilitator, when I hear people say, "I don't care about people, money, making a difference, material things, clothes, nice jewelry," my ears perk up and I start asking questions. People often say these things because they don't believe they can have it or deserve it. People often say these things when they don't like their current results in that area or when they feel like it is out of their control to produce a different result. They have already counted themselves out of having x, y, or z.

Remember the whipped cream you slather on to justify your current results? You say these things in order to be okay with your current results so you don't have to change. If I said I cared a great deal about money and money is important, yet I was broke, I've created a discrepancy. Therefore, a tension is created—a tension that must be resolved. I can resolve it by changing my results and making money or I can convince myself and everyone else that I don't care about money and keep doing what I am doing. The latter is easier than the former. People who have money don't say, "I don't care about money."

Sometimes people say that they don't care about x, y, or z because they don't realize the consequences of x, y, or z on their self-esteem or future opportunities. It's common to say, "I don't care about clothes," not realizing that the way you dress is greatly affecting your self-esteem and who you project to the world. It's easy to say, "I don't care about being late," not realizing that being late affects your income, your level of respect, future opportunities, your relationships, and your self-esteem.

Start thinking about the things that you do or don't do that chip away at your self-esteem. When you start beating yourself up, what is it about? Where do you experience shame or guilt? What do you nag yourself about? One of mine is the dentist.

If I put off making an appointment with the dentist, there's that voice inside my head that says, "When are you going to get that dentist appointment handled? That really should have been last month. You probably have 17 cavities and your teeth are going to fall out, and then you'll have to get dentures. You really messed up."

The nagging just goes on and on in my head, taking hits on my self-esteem every time I think about it until I make that appointment. Now, when I make the appointment, the stress I've been putting myself under decreases, and the negative things I am saying to myself lessen. Therefore, the hits on my self-esteem lessen. When I actually go to the appointment, I walk out afterwards feeling light and free, as if I won the lottery!

Everything feels good because I have now done an action that increased my self-esteem and stopped the inaction that decreased my self-esteem. Now, the voice inside my head says, "Check me out! I have no cavities! I have the cleanest mouth in the world! We should celebrate!" I am no longer experiencing distressing thoughts, and I also feel good about taking care of something that is important to me.

List 10 things you do that decrease your self-esteem (self-esteem chippers):

1. _____
2. _____
3. _____
4. _____
5. _____
6. _____
7. _____
8. _____
9. _____
10. _____

List 10 things you do that increase your self-esteem (self-esteem boosters):

1. _____
2. _____
3. _____
4. _____
5. _____
6. _____
7. _____
8. _____
9. _____
10. _____

SELF-ESTEEM BANK ACCOUNT

Your self-esteem is similar to a bank account. On day one, your account balance is zero. Let's pretend that during the day you do 50 things to increase your self-esteem, and you do 25 things to decrease or chip away at your self-esteem. At the end of the day, you have a net positive balance of 25. Even though the majority of these 75 things are unconscious, everything you think, do, or say counts.

On day two, maybe you've netted another positive 25. That means you're up to 50—overall—when combining both days. Unfortunately, when day three comes along, you have a bad day. You end the day netting a negative 25. Now, your overall balance is back to a net of 25. Over time, those days turn into weeks, which average into future months and, eventually, years.

After 10 years, you've got 3,650 days of balances that have accumulated. Your self-esteem *today* is simply the result of the accumulation of *the last 3,650 days*. And 10 years from now, your self-esteem will be the result of the accumulation of the next 3,650 days. Over 3,650 days, you will have days that are mega-high (10%) and days that are mega-low (10%).

Like the stock market, there are huge plummets and major gains. Sure, they make a difference in the overall picture and in the moment, but the stock market settles back to the average of the many other days in between, where minor gains and losses occur (80%). There is nothing magical about 10 years, I am simply using that number as a unit of time to make a point. What you did yesterday contributes. What you did 50 years ago contributes.

"How you did things today is not your problem. It was the 3,650 days that came before today."

- RENEE CERMAK -

TWO WOLVES: A CHEROKEE LEGEND

*An old Cherokee was teaching his granddaughter about life.
"A fight is going on inside me," he said to the girl.*

*"It is a terrible fight, and it is between two wolves. One is evil—he is anger,
envy, sorrow, regret, greed, arrogance, self-pity, guilt, resentment, inferiority, lies,
false pride, superiority, and ego." He continued, "The other is good—he is joy,
peace, love, hope, serenity, humility, kindness, benevolence, empathy, generosity,
truth, compassion, and faith. The same fight is going on inside you—and inside
every other person, too."*

*The granddaughter thought about it for a minute and then asked her grandfather,
"Which wolf will win?"*

The old Cherokee simply replied, "The one you feed."

As another example, consider that you have two piles of evidence
in your life. One pile is full of evidence of your limiting beliefs—you
can't, you're not enough, you don't deserve it. While the other is filled
with evidence of your non-limiting beliefs—you can, you are enough,
you do deserve it. Whichever pile of evidence is bigger is the one that's
going to take over when you go on autopilot or when you rely on your

subconscious—which, for most people, can be about 95% of the time.

As far as I have seen, there is no neutral pile; you're either putting evidence in the "can do" pile (self-esteem boosters), or you're putting evidence into the "can't do" pile (self-esteem chippers).

Once you are aware of this dynamic and its effect on your self-esteem, every day can be a new day. Each day, you can ask yourself, "Which wolf am I going to feed?" Maybe yesterday you fed the wolf of gossip and jealousy. Well, today is a new day to wipe the slate clean! If you can add up enough days of feeding the wolf of generosity, compassion, and love, the good wolf will overpower the other one, and you will win.

> "The grass is not, in fact, always greener on the other side of the fence. Fences have nothing to do with it. The grass is greenest where it is watered. When crossing over fences, carry water with you and tend the grass wherever you may be."
>
> - ROBERT FULGHUM -

This may come as a surprise to you, but you only need to be "winning" 51% of the time. Isn't that a relief? You don't need to be perfect. It's okay if you find you can't feed the good wolf 100% of the time. Even if you've spent days, weeks, months, or years feeding the other wolf, you can still turn it around and create something different. It just starts with taking one step and taking one day at a time. It will not happen overnight, but with each step, you move closer to what you want.

If you have spent 20 years giving yourself evidence that you are not enough, then start today to give yourself evidence that you *are* enough. If you have spent 20 years eating the wrong food to give yourself evidence that you are unhealthy, then start today to make different choices to commit to your health. If you look at your life in terms of one day at a time, then think of all the small stuff that you can turn from negative to positive. Remember: if you can master the small stuff, you're more likely to handle the big things in life with grace and ease.

> "The Chinese say, 'The best time to plant a tree was always 20 years ago. The second best time is always today.' Funny how planting trees and taking action on the life of your dreams are the same that way."
>
> - THE UNIVERSE -

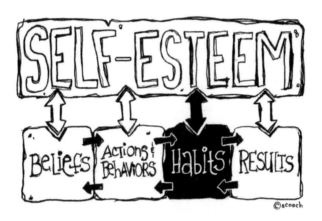

GETTING CONSCIOUS ABOUT YOUR HABITS

When we talk about doing the small stuff over and over, day after day, what are we really talking about? Habits. If you repeat the same actions and behaviors long enough, they become habits. You and I are just huge collections of habits.

The majority of what we do, how we do it, and how we experience it are just habits. Most of what we do, from the moment we wake up to the moment we go to bed, is a habit. Most of these habits are unconscious, too. Our beliefs—the beliefs we formed as young children—create actions and behaviors which, over time, form our habits. Habits create results.

Wouldn't it be valuable to explore the habits that are creating *your* results—especially the habits you are doing day in and day out without even being conscious of them? Your habits are just a way you learned how to do things not necessarily the right way, the best way, or the only way—just one way. Once you figured out "your way," you adopted it as the right way.

You get accustomed to your way of doing things, and you like other people to do it that way, too. You like to be right about your way because you are invested in it. Yet, your way is simply one way out of hundreds of options. Usually, it is not the fastest or most effective way. It is definitely not the right way; it is just your way. It's a habit.

The quickest way to create your extraordinary future is to give up your way. The quickest way to achieve goals is to give up your way. The easiest way to create great relationships is to give up your way. Instead of being committed to your way, be committed to the end result: the extraordinary future, the goal, the great relationship. In focusing on the end result versus your way, the mechanism, you open yourself up to solutions, resources, and opportunities that your way might not include. When you create your extraordinary life, whatever that looks like to you, do you think you'll care how many times you did it your way or her way or his way? Do you think you'll care how many times you were right?

Giving up your way = Giving up control = Surrender = Committed to the end result = Open to any solution = Bliss

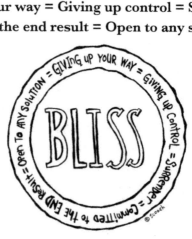

Most people don't realize that in giving up control, one has much more control. Some people think giving up control is a bad thing and don't realize their need for control is suffocating new possibilities and solutions and cutting off ways to succeed. They don't realize when you surrender "your way" that a whole new world opens up. The truth is when we understand that the "looser the grip, the tighter the hold" we create very different results. Your way is simply a habit. The good news is if you learned one way, you can learn a different way.

- Doing things immediately is a habit, as is procrastinating.

- Doing things your way is a habit, as is being flexible and being open to new ideas.

- Arriving late is a habit, as is arriving on time.

- Paying bills on time is a habit, as is paying late fees.

- Being patient and kind is a habit, as is being impatient and rude.

- Networking is a habit, as is sitting on your couch.

- Being reactive and defensive is a habit, as is listening.

Certain unconscious habits are necessary. Otherwise, it would take forever to get anything accomplished. At one point in time you were conscious about tying your shoes and now it is a habit that you've handed off to your subconscious mind. You tie your shoes the same way every time.

Think about driving. At one point, you were conscious about every part of driving—accelerating, shifting gears, slowing down, merging. You even used to use turn signals. Then, you said, "I don't have time to be conscious about driving while driving! I can eat, change the music, talk..." and that's when you handed the driving off to your subconscious—just like plenty of other things you do. Have you ever driven home, pulled in your driveway, and had no idea how you got there? Who drove?

We have handed off thousands of things to our subconscious that show up in the form of habits. We do this to be efficient. If we are going to do it the same way every time, why bother thinking about it?

Shoe tying and driving are good examples of habits to leave with your subconscious mind. However, there are habits that are very dangerous to hand off to your subconscious. There are places in your life where doing something the same way every time would be a poor choice. We have often even handed off habits like parenting and how to handle conflict to our subconscious. Instead of being conscious about our parenting, choosing how to be with our children, what to say and how to respond, we often rely on habits that may not be fostering an exceptional relationship.

The same is true of how we handle conflict. Instead of being conscious about how we would like to respond, we often have an unconscious habit about how to react. Typical unconscious (knee-jerk) reactions include anger, blame, justification, avoidance, and denial. None of these reactions are effective ways to handle conflict. Being responsible means having the ability to respond. In order to be able to respond, you actually must be conscious in the moment of response.

BUILDING SUPERHIGHWAYS

How are these habits formed? All of this is happening in your brain through neural pathways. Think of the neurons in your brain as telephone wires connecting thoughts. When you were born, all you had were the "basic trunk lines...connecting one city to another, but the specific connections from one house to another require additional signals" (Gopnick). Then you started learning skills, watching your parents, repeating actions until you mastered them, and building more pathways. Over time, you build and unbuild all of those connections based on use.

> At birth, each neuron in the cerebral cortex has approximately 2,500 synapses. By the time an infant is 2 or 3, the number of synapses is approximately 15,000 synapses per neuron. As we age, old connections are deleted through a process called synaptic pruning. Synaptic pruning eliminates weaker synaptic contacts, while stronger connections are kept and strengthened. Experience determines which connections will be strengthened, and which will be pruned; connections that have been activated most frequently are preserved. Neurons must have a purpose to survive (Gopnick).

Your habits are those strong connections. They were *learned* behaviors—you were not born with them. Imagine these neural pathways are roads. When you were born, there were very few roads—mostly jungle everywhere. You were a pioneer making your way through the jungle.

You learned that certain actions got you what you wanted—milk, food, attention, toys. And you were willing to do them over and over in order to get better. That's how you learned to grab things, how you learned to walk, and how you learned to talk. With enough repetition, you create a path through the jungle. If you walk that path long enough, over and over, it gets wider and easier to navigate and eventually turns into a dirt road. If you walk that dirt road long enough, it becomes a paved road. If you drive that paved road long enough, it becomes wider and, soon, it is easy to create a second lane. Pretty soon, you are driving down a four-lane superhighway: smooth, wide, easy, comfortable, and effortless; especially when compared to a dirt road, path, or even the jungle.

Let's look at a four-year-old and how they get attention. They could choose to get attention through good behavior, bad behavior, being silent, performing, being needy, wetting the bed, being shy, breaking things, being sick, hitting other kids, being funny, not getting clothes dirty, and the list goes on. Chances are they are going to go down many of these paths. Some they will turn into dirt roads, and some into superhighways. Their superhighways are their habits. Think about some of the ways you get attention today. You might be driving down superhighways created by a four-year-old. Remember learning how to tie your shoes? It is highly likely you still tie your shoes the exact same way you learned when you were four. It is a superhighway. What else are you doing the exact same way you learned as a four-year-old?

Recently, I had the opportunity to spend time with some friends and their kids —three kids from different families. When it was time for dinner, they didn't want to stop playing with the iPad. During dinner, they would sneak over to the iPad and press the buttons. Every time they did this, I would shout to the room the number of infractions they had. "That's 10 times you touched the iPad when you were told not to." They got the number up to 20 pretty fast. So, in order to get the iPad back after dinner, they had to do 20 "nice" actions.

It was interesting to see the different responses from the kids. One little girl was not participating, so I asked her if she could tell her aunt something nice that she appreciates. She came into my embrace really close and whispered, "I can't. Actually, I am shy." My first thought was, "I wonder who told you that?" What I said was, "Okay, you can be shy and do nice things, too. Go tell your aunt."

In thinking back about my past experiences with this child, I realized that being shy was one of the ways she got attention. That day, she was using her shyness to get attention and to be incapable. At seven years old, she was already counting herself out of the game because of her neural pathways—her superhighway directing her to be shy.

With enough repetition, all of the small stuff you do will create a pathway in your brain that becomes stronger and stronger and, eventually, the repeated ways of thinking and behaviors become habitual. It wasn't just one moment in time, one thought, or one action that formed that pathway; it was the result of days, weeks, months, and years of repetitive thoughts and behaviors that allowed that positive (or negative) neural road to become established.

The majority of the superhighways (your habits) you travel on today as an adult were created when you were still *a child*. Again, when you are willing to be aware, you uncover your beliefs and habits and you can make changes. You can turn superhighways back into dirt roads. You can turn dirt roads into superhighways. The choice is yours.

Based on these habits, your actions and reactions become very predictable: when life happens, when a situation presents itself, or when one of your buttons gets pushed, you go on autopilot; you don't have to think. Why? Because there is always a clear choice in your brain based on past choices. It's the neural pathway with the biggest, widest, most drivable and manageable road—it's the superhighway, saying, "Pick me, pick me! You've always picked me! I am what you know. I am your go-to guy. I am a four-lane superhighway. Look at those dirt roads over there, bumpy and dirty, very inconvenient. Look at those paths; you don't have time for that. I am safe, comfortable, fast, and easy."

Some of your highways have even added big neon signs, just in case. You have a typical way you handle conflict, spend money—you have built a superhighway for everything you do. Even though there are 100 other roads to get there, you predominantly use your one road because it's what you know.

Have you ever met someone who has an angry button? When *that* button gets pushed, they go from zero to 60 mph in seconds, every time. Clearly, there are other ways to handle whatever happened, but they can't see it. Their reaction is automatic. Consider your computer and default settings. A default setting is "a selection automatically used by a computer program in the absence of a choice made by the user." Also, "a selection made usually automatically or without active consideration due to lack of a viable alternative."

You, too, have default settings for everything. Resistance is a default setting. Somebody pushes, and you automatically push back. You operate from your default settings the majority of the time. This is not a bad thing, and this will never change. What can change, however, is your default settings.

Your job is to become curious about you and all of your reactions (default settings); becoming fascinated is even better. When someone pushes your buttons and you react, be willing to ask questions to uncover why. Out of all the possible reactions, why did you choose that one? What is it about the person or the subject or the situation that you don't like? What belief of yours has been challenged? When we ask questions, we get answers.

In the answers, you can make discoveries about your unconscious belief and operating systems. Then you can see that there is simply another belief out there rubbing against yours, a different viewpoint. Once you realize this, then you can take control versus walking away or wanting it to stop. With answers, you gain the power to no longer let it bother you or cause you to react. It was never about the other person. Your job is to minimize the amount of buttons that control you.

"Whatever you resist is in control of you. If someone is able to push your buttons, then you have not yet reached mastery in that area."

- COURTLAND WARREN -

Neural plasticity means the neural pathways in the brain are always changing based on repetition and experience. Targeted neural pathways can be strengthened. New paths can be formed, dirt roads can be paved, and paved roads can become highways. At the same time, synaptic pruning means synaptic contacts can be eliminated. If you don't use it, you can lose it.

It's like putting up a detour sign. You can cut off all access permanently to a four-lane superhighway and, eventually, it will go back to a dirt road. Think about people who quit smoking: they unpaved a superhighway and turned the "smoking" road back into a jungle.

You can decide which roads to use. There is no good or bad or right or wrong road when it comes to neural pathways. The real question is, "How are your four-lane superhighways working out for you?" Remember, you have as many as 100 to 1,000 choices, depending on the situation. What if you were more committed to a way that works instead of *your way?*

CREATING NEW SUPERHIGHWAYS

"Thinking small isn't easy or hard. It's just a habit.
A habit with consequences.
Same for thinking big. God, I love these things..."

- THE UNIVERSE -

So, how do you create new habits? Easily—the same way you created the old habits—through repetition of the small stuff. With a focus on the small things, you will be able to create new habits made of different actions and behaviors, creating higher self-esteem and bigger, better results.

Your self-esteem and the little things you do or don't do are inextricably wound together to produce the results that surround you, big and small, in *every* area of your life. The more times you do something consistently, the more it will add to your self-esteem, building a habit. More importantly, it will build an *I am* statement, impacting your belief system.

Imagine that you live paycheck to paycheck or that as soon as you get money it seems to slip through your fingers, leaving you with none. You might be saying to yourself on a daily basis, "I am broke. I am not good with money." Every day you are chipping away at your self-esteem. Then, you decide to use the simplest wealth building tool out there: paying yourself 10% first. That means that when money comes in, 10% immediately moves to your savings account. You use the 90% that is left to live and pay your bills. If you ask most people about this tool, they could speak about it, understand it, yet few actually use it. Can you imagine how much money would be in that savings account if you had saved 10% of what you made since you were 18 years old?

Every paycheck, you transfer 10% over to your savings account. After a while, you have a few hundred dollars. After a number of months, you have a few thousand dollars. And now your *I am* statements start to change. "I have money. I can save."

After a couple years, saving 10% is a habit. Those small daily actions build up over time. Imagine the first month you saved 10% versus a month in your second or third year. When you do something for years, it becomes more powerful. It becomes who you are versus what you do. The amount of pride you'll build will keep you moving forward. That's the thing about doing things to help your self-esteem. It's addictive, but in a good way. The better you do, the more you save, the higher your self-esteem goes up. Don't you want that?

- Imagine how you feel the first year you tithe 10% of your income versus how you feel the 10th year you tithe.

- Or the first time you raised money for a charity compared to the 20th.

- Or the first day you took supplements compared to the 300th.

- Or the first time you took the high road compared to the 50th.

- Or the first time you drove a car compared to the 300th.

- Or the first year you worked somewhere compared to the fifth.

- Or the first year you were sober compared to the 20th.

- Do you want to go with me the first time I fly a plane? No? What about the 500th?

Every time you do a repeated action, you gain more evidence that it is not bigger than you. You achieve bigger results, you find your niche, and, most importantly, you change your *I am* statements.

Some people say you're "lucky" or "unlucky." An extraordinary life has nothing to do with luck. Instead, your life is just a collection of all those little things that build up over time in a very powerful way and create a great self-esteem or not. Build your own *I am* statements. What are the *I am* statements you want to have? What do you want to say about yourself? What are the small things that will get you there? Do them over and over and over. Get committed to the hundredth time.

What are five new habits that you will create?

1. _____

2. _____

3. _____

4. _____

5. _____

Your repeated actions and behaviors day after day build into habits. Your habits, week after week, month after month, year after year, will culminate into a series of results. When you are 90 years old and looking back (if you do the daily small stuff to live to be 90 years old), there will be significant results staring back at you. Will they be the results that you want?

There might be 10 things that will stand out as the very marrow of your life. Decide what you want those 10 things to be and get committed to the small actions that will get you there. Decide what you want to be known for. Decide what you want people to say at your funeral, and then create that narrative. None of it has to be left to chance. I know, for the most part, what people will say at my funeral, because I have decided and am committed to those things on a daily basis. What about you?

In the end, will people say you were an exceptional parent, significant other, and friend? That you were unreasonable, abnormal, and uncommon? Will you be known as someone who made things happen, who had a great attitude, and who was willing to work hard?

At your funeral, will people stand up and say you led by example and took responsibility for your actions and results? That you took a stand for yourself and your values? That you were passionate, courageous, generous, and influential? Will they say you were committed to your integrity? Will everyone agree that you made a difference? That because of how you lived hundreds—maybe thousands—of people were better off?

None of these results will simply happen. People who are known for these things put a great deal of time, discipline, and attention into the small stuff. And it all starts with one decision and one action. What do you want your life to say? What results do you really want?

CHAPTER 4
RESULTS

❝ When I first started working in real estate, my average sale was $150,000. I grew up in a middle class home, and getting a paycheck for $2,000 or more was a lot of money. I shared an office with a friend, and one day she sold a $2 million dollar house. I couldn't even wrap my brain around receiving a paycheck for $60,000!

Once I learned about self-esteem and results, I knew I had to work on mine. I wanted to work smarter, not harder, and was tired of working so hard for small commissions, as they also affected my self-worth. I learned that knowledge will build a person's self-esteem, so I was determined to learn about luxury homes and the clientele I wanted to serve.

I read books, went to luxury home tours, and networked with the agents doing that type of work. Within a year, I had my first luxury listing at $4 million in Paradise Valley, AZ. During that time, I took full advantage of having this listing. I had parties and made calls, which led to friendships and invitations to the most elite homes.

Once the house sold, my self-esteem had grown to a level where I realized there are no limits. I really could do anything I put my mind to. I have continued on this self-esteem journey every day. I've run five marathons, become a foster parent, and now lead the #1 real estate team in our office, with over $60 million per year in sales. Every step counts, and we don't get there alone. **"**

-Jenny McCall

You produce results 24 hours a day. You produce good results and bad results, effective results and ineffective results; you may achieve 97% of your goals or you may achieve 42% of your goals. You are not able to get away from your results; they are everywhere.

> "Every choice you make has an end result."
>
> - ZIG ZIGLAR -

There are many contributors to your results. In chapter two, we looked at how your beliefs create the foundation for all future results. Your beliefs also dictate your actions and behaviors. In chapter three, we looked at how the small stuff, your actions and behaviors over time, form habits.

In this chapter, we will look at how your habits, doing the same thing over and over again, produce significant results both good and bad.

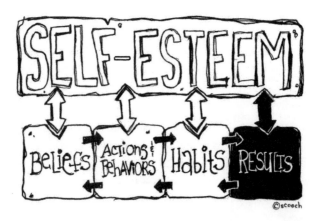

CREDIT SCORE

One of those results is your credit score. Your credit score is a great example of how small things over time have created your current financial habits and have netted you a meaningful result. Your credit score has been created moment by moment, purchase by purchase, and payment by payment for the last seven years (at minimum).

Thousands of pieces of data over years and years have been used to track your financial actions and behaviors (the small stuff); these thousands of pieces come together into *one* tangible number. Your credit score affects multiple aspects of your life; it affects your ability to rent or purchase a home or car and the interest rate you pay for those loans. It can also impact your insurance rates and your ability to make other major purchases.

Your credit score can impact whether you get the job or security clearance. A higher credit score makes life easier and saves you money. So, how does one number come to mean so much? It's the 10,000 small things that are behind the one number.

- How many late payments?
- How many missed payments?
- How many credit inquiries?
- Who is inquiring?
- How much debt do you carry?
- Current balances compared to the limit?
- Bankruptcy?
- Collections?
- How have you handled debt in the past?
- How long have you had credit?

This one number tells creditors whether you are a good bet or not. The higher your score, the better bet you are, and the more likely you are to pay your debts.

- A score between 500 and 600 means one out of every eight people will default on their debts.

- A score of 800 means that one out of every 1,292 people will default on their debts.

Based on what? Past behavior predicts current and future behavior.

What is your credit score? Do you know it? _____

If you want to see the results of your financial thinking, behaviors, and actions, the two best places to look are your credit score and net worth. So, if you don't know your credit score and net worth, what could that mean about you and your financial beliefs? If you have a credit score in the 500s, what could that mean about you and your financial beliefs and habits?

REPUTATION SCORE

The *same* thing holds true with your reputation. Your current reputation has been created moment by moment over the last 10, 20, 30 years. You have a reputation score just like you have a credit score, only it is invisible. Yet, it is just as valid of a measuring tool as your credit score. Ten thousand pieces of information regarding your past actions and behaviors (*the small stuff*) come together to form one *invisible* number.

Why is your reputation score important? Your reputation score affects even more areas of your life than a credit score. Your reputation—how people view you— affects how you view yourself.

Your reputation affects whether people want to hire you, buy from you, partner with you, or steal from you—which affects your financial results. Results impact your self-esteem.

Your reputation affects whether people want to befriend you, date you, commit with you, or just have sex with you—which affects your relationship results. Results impact your self-esteem. Your reputation affects your ability to influence, inspire, and make a difference, which affects your self-esteem.

So, what's behind this reputation score?

- How many times were you on time? Or late?
- How many times did you do what you said you were going to do? Or didn't?
- How many times were you helpful and supportive? Or not?
- How many times did you take a stand? Or didn't?
- How many times did you apologize? Or didn't?
- How many times did you compromise? Or didn't?

You have a reputation with your significant other, kids, boss, coworkers, friends—with *everyone*. Every one of them could give you an accurate score between zero and 100 right now. People decide what you are about through your actions and behavior. People are betting on you every day: your kids, your boss, your employees, your significant other, your community.

> "Who you are speaks so loudly I can't hear a word you're saying."
> - RALPH WALDO EMERSON -

The question is, *how are they betting*? Are they betting that, once again, you won't be home for dinner as promised? Are they betting that you will meet the deadline as usual? Are they betting that you will be dependable? Flaky? Positive? Negative? Do you have a reputation of being a gossip, a victim, a complainer, or a long storyteller?

Or maybe you have a reputation of paying attention to detail, being a great friend, or being loyal. Do you have a reputation of speaking the truth, being the life of the party, or being a drag? Your reputation scores with some people are made up of five pieces of information because you met them just last week. Your reputation scores with other people may be made up of 10,000 pieces of information because you have a 40-year relationship.

This information might come in the form of personal experiences, experiences they witness, or even experiences they only hear about. It all adds up. People seem clueless to the fact that the way they are today affects their reputation and how many people want to work and play with them in the future.

> "What if you received an award...for every moment of your life, for whatever you did or didn't do?
>
> Yeah, that's pretty much the case. Bravo, bravo!!"
>
> - THE UNIVERSE -

What score would your significant other give you? _____

What score would your children give you? _____

What score would your coworkers/colleagues give you? _____

What score would your employees/employers give you? _____

Most importantly, you have a reputation with *yourself*. You could give yourself an accurate reputation score right now. You know what your number is—just look in the mirror. This is important because the reputation you have with yourself is a huge contributor to your overall self-esteem, just as ALL results in your life are a reflection of your self-esteem.

What is your reputation score with yourself? _____

Maybe you don't like some of these numbers you've written down so far. The great news is that you can start changing your reputation today, just like your self-esteem, by concentrating on the small stuff.

More great news: it may have taken you 10 years to create your current, not-so-great reputation with someone—say a score in the 60s. If you are aware, focused, and purposeful, it may take you only a year to get that reputation score up into the 90s. If you have an 11-year relationship with someone, the last year carries markedly more weight than the first. What are things that you could do to improve your reputation with these people? With all people? It's never too late.

> "Saints are sinners who kept on going."
> - ROBERT LOUIS STEVENSON -

Think about your clients and customers. What reputation score would they give you? What if you wrote down all of your clients and the corresponding reputation score you think you have with them? Think about your clients who might give you scores in the 70s and 80s. What could you do tomorrow to improve your reputation with them? What are five actions you could take to get that score in the 90s?

Think about a new group or person you have started associating with in the last year. You have developed a reputation with them over the past 365 days. Have they decided that you are authentic, positive, solution-oriented, flexible, committed to results, a leader, play a big game, and do what you say you are going to do? Or have they decided that you are not dependable, are condescending, not open to solutions, out of integrity, play a small game, allow obstacles to stop you, or something in between? Some of you will say, "I don't care about those people."

Well, there are other people who feel the same way—people who you *do* care about. Because what you do in one relationship is what you do in most relationships. If you like to exaggerate, do you only exaggerate in some relationships? Likely not. If you are authentic, are you authentic in only some of your friendships? Likely not. Everyone you meet will decide whether they would hire you or partner with you, date you, or be friends with you—and you will do the same.

Why should you care what they think if your vote is the only one that matters? Because your behaviors and habits impact you, too— not just these relationships. It is impossible to have poor reputation scores all across your life and feel good about yourself, because you know all the small stuff that created those results. The best example of this is your reputation as a parent. If you know your child would give you a low score right now, you also know that you would give yourself that same low score. If you habitually lose your temper with your child, you both lose. You both score yourself low. The results of where you stand with people are *always* a reflection of your own standing with yourself.

Pick five people in your **personal** life that you would like to have a better reputation with. What are five things that you could start/ stop doing for each one to improve your score?

Person 1. Five things I could start/stop doing to improve my reputation score with _____:

1. _____

2. _____

3. _____

4. _____

5. _____

Person 2. Five things I could start/stop doing to improve my reputation score with _____:

1. _____

2. _____

3. _____

4. _____

5. _____

Person 3. Five things I could start/stop doing to improve my reputation score with _____:

1. _____

2. _____

3. _____

4. _____

5. _____

Person 4. Five things I could start/stop doing to improve my reputation score with _____:

1. _____

2. _____

3. _____

4. _____

5. _____

Person 5. Five things I could start/stop doing to improve my reputation score with _____:

1. _____

2. _____

3. _____

4. _____

5. _____

Pick five people in your **professional** life that you would like to have a better reputation with. What are five things that you could start/stop doing for each one to improve your score?

Person 1. Five things I could start/stop doing to improve my reputation score with _____:

1. _____

2. _____

3. _____

4. _____

5. _____

Person 2. Five things I could start/stop doing to improve my reputation score with _____:

1. _____

2. _____

3. _____

4. _____

5. _____

Person 3. Five things I could start/stop doing to improve my reputation score with _____:

1. _____

2. _____

3. _____

4. _____

5. _____

Person 4. Five things I could start/stop doing to improve my reputation score with _____:

1. _____

2. _____

3. _____

4. _____

5. _____

Person 5. Five things I could start/stop doing to improve my reputation score with _____:

1. _____

2. _____

3. _____

4. _____

5. _____

RELATIONSHIP RESULTS

Relationships that fail are typically the result of days, weeks, months, and years of small criticisms, complaints, and arguments. It wasn't just one comment or infraction that ended the relationship; it was the accumulation of continual negativity over time. On the flip side, phenomenal partnerships are the product of many, many small interactions that accumulate one by one and, over time, become the foundation of a positive, strong relationship.

I walked in my closet one day and noticed a whole pile of clean clothes in the wrong spot on a shelf. It immediately became clear that my husband had folded laundry. My first thought was, "Couldn't you take the next step and put the clothes away?" I was about to shout something derogatory to my husband when a little voice in my head said, "Can we please celebrate the fact that he folded the laundry?" And one more point: "*You* don't even know where to put your clean laundry; this place is a mess. How could he possibly figure it out? Imagine if he put it in the wrong spot, you'd be complaining about that." I immediately thanked my husband for folding the laundry. Sometimes I catch myself; sometimes I don't.

> "You can have great relationships or you can be right, not both."
> - TIM O'KELLEY -

Every time I choose to nitpick at my husband, I am contributing to our marriage. Every time I choose to express my gratitude to my husband, I am contributing to our marriage. It is my responsibility to catch myself more often. Every time I take that one small step to be cognizant of how I communicate, I contribute to a more open, trusting dialogue. Partners who spend their time building each other up through words and deeds ensure the relationship will be successful in the long run. It's not a magic formula; it is simply the natural by-product of all of the "little things" adding up over time.

Everything you choose to do (or not do) will have an effect. Keeping your mouth shut when you want to criticize, not always having to be right, taking an interest in your significant other's hobbies, apologizing often, making compromises over where you go on vacation—*all* of these will add up to a great relationship over time.

The reverse is true as well: giving your significant other the silent treatment, withholding sex, blaming, always having to be "right," spending above your means—*all* of these actions will lead to the demise of the relationship over time.

> "When you are wrong, admit it immediately.
> When you are right, zip it."
>
> - TIM O'KELLEY -

66 Regarding focusing on the end result versus being right, in my marriage one of the end results I remain focused on is, 'All I want is to see Michelle happy.' This little phrase has served me time after time. Anytime there is miscommunication or conflict between us, I always start the process of resolution in my mind with that phrase. It quickly lays the foundation for me to find the bridge that will allow us to get connected once again. If all I want is for her to be happy, then letting go of being right is easier to do. **99**

- Matt Moses

FOR THE SAKE OF WHAT

About 20 years ago I was in facilitator training, and I learned a profound life tool from the lead trainer, Kelly Poulos. Forty of us were practicing speaking and teaching material from the front of the room, and Kelly was coaching us. In the middle of his talk, she stopped a man named Jeff and asked, "For the sake of what are you speaking right now?" He didn't know how to answer her question. She said, "There is a reason that you said x, y, and z. What is it?" He still didn't know what she meant. It took her five more minutes and rephrasing the question three more times before his light bulb lit up. He finally realized that the reason he said what he said was to be right, not to teach something, not to connect with the audience. Simply to be right. And then Kelly pointed out that being more committed to being right than to teaching and connecting as a facilitator is not good. I have never forgotten that moment. *"For the sake of what are you speaking right now?"* There are many reasons why we open our mouth and speak. Sometimes it is to be right, to make someone else wrong, to be better than, to look good, or to criticize. Sometimes we use humor when we are uncomfortable to avoid and to deflect. Sometimes we speak to teach, to connect, to love, or to give a compliment. Sometimes we speak to share, to support, to cheerlead, or to take a stand.

If you are about to speak, take three seconds to think about, *"For the sake of what am I about to speak?"* If it is for good, start talking. If it is not, maybe zip it. This is a valuable tool because you not only get to really understand and know *yourself*, you get to improve your relationship with *anyone* you practice this with.

Your relationship with your children is also built on small moments over a long distance. My mother is still as committed to family gatherings and traditions as she was when I was growing up. She has been consistent for 55 years. My mom has six kids: five girls and one boy. Her identical twin sister also has six kids: five girls and one boy.

My mom and aunt were committed to their 12 children spending as much time together as possible, including every holiday. They had multiple obstacles to their commitment: living in different states, complaining children, life with six kids, and the huge inconvenience. Imagine the amount of time, energy, planning, cooking, driving, and cleaning it took to make these special occasions happen. And then know that they were both patient, giving, and loving women through it all. See how easy it would be for me to give my mom a high reputation score?

I remember going on a day trip, including a nice boat ride, to see George Washington's house. Every child complained the entire time. Now, with my own child, I am even more aware of the time and energy and years of consistency that are required for me to build a long-lasting and meaningful relationship.

Being a parent is the ultimate giving experience. You know your kids will not fully appreciate you until much later, around the time that you fully appreciated your parents. You know your child is going to watch you, judge you, throw zingers at you, and condemn you. The relationship with a child is set up to be tested, to be challenging, to come back full circle several times. There are too many small things to count that parents are willing to do that kids do not appreciate at the time:

- Being their chauffer, their cook, their cleaning person.
- Taking them on educational outings.
- Keeping traditions: religious, cultural, family.
- Going to game after game, or play after play.
- Taking care of their many illnesses.
- Making each meal happen.

Yet, parents are willing to do a myriad of small things daily to raise their children with love and consistency. These actions add up day after day.

Remember, negative actions add up, too. Not listening to your child, not spending time with him, not following through with your promise to play catch, yelling, criticizing, not enforcing boundaries, or lying all add up to a relationship that is not as full or loving as it could be. All those times you stayed late at work and missed the piano recital, or dismissed your child's needs, also add up—just not in a positive direction.

These illustrations are not meant to make you feel guilty but to help you realize that all of the little actions that may seem insignificant do make a difference, especially in the life of a child. You may be surprised at the tiniest details that your child will forever remember fondly, so don't discount the small things, thinking that relationships are only built during milestone events and years.

The daily interactions between parent and child affect their self-esteem as well as yours. If you are a parent, then what you do as a parent, say as a parent, and how you behave as parent will most definitely affect your self-esteem. More importantly, how you evaluate yourself as a parent affects your self-estimate.

Have you ever gone to *Schmuckville*? I came home one day to find my husband and my daughter both in low moods. I asked what was wrong. My husband said, "Oh, I went to Schmuckville." I asked him what that meant. He said, "I learned it from a guy at the gym. It's when you lose your temper and do and say things to your children that you regret later." I, too, have been to Schmuckville. Every time I go to Schmuckville, the self-esteem chippers come out. Every time I say we will do it later, and we don't, my self-esteem is affected. Every time I give her only 70%, we both know.

Every day that my child gets to school on time happy, healthy, clean, and with a good lunch, my self-esteem gets a little boost. Two days a week at 8:00 a.m. swim class, as I watch my daughter become pool safe and an amazing swimmer, my self-esteem increases. Every time I give her 100%, both of our self-esteems soar.

When our self-esteems soar, beautiful things happen. A strong bond is created when your child feels loved and supported. It gives them the foundation they need to start feeding their self-esteem early on.

PHYSICAL RESULTS

Your physical body is a visual, undeniable presentation to the world of your self-esteem. When you look at the whole of how you arrived at your current level of health, it can be quite overwhelming. Let's look at the last 10 years, or 3,650 days. Each one of these 3,650 days you have had nearly endless choices. You made literally thousands of choices daily.

The small stuff here is obvious: each meal, each snack, each exercise, each drink, each doctor's appointment kept or missed. Those habits created measurable results: one number is how much you weigh, one number is your cholesterol, one number is your body fat percentage, and on and on. You can choose to view all these measures as overwhelming or view them all as opportunities to make changes.

The majority of people come into this world with perfect health. I am not referring to people who do not. If we were to check in with every human being at age 20, there would be a huge variation in health results. We could do the same check-in at age 30, at age 40, and at age 50 and see even wider differences. When we check in at age 50, after a whole lifetime of choices, there are significantly different results than when we were born and when we checked in at 20 years old.

For the most part, people believe that certain actions lead to certain health results. I don't think there is anyone who would deny that smoking cigarettes causes lung diseases. If we were to look at each person's health results at age 50, and then looked at their history of diet, exercise, sleep, doctor appointments kept or not kept, we would be able to make some correlations.

We all get to look at what we did with our opportunity in these bodies, taking into consideration our own genetics. We all created something different with our opportunity. I recently saw an interesting image on Facebook featuring two women. The caption read, "Both of these women are 74 years old. The choice is yours." One of the women was in a wheelchair; the other just finished a fitness contest.

All of the results in your life are fundamental to your self-esteem. Your results inform you how you feel about you. People with phenomenal self-worth have great results—in every part of their lives: their reputation with themselves and others, their financial health, their relationships, their physical health, their minds, and their contribution to society. Because what you do here is what you do there is what you do everywhere. It's a mindset.

Your results create your self-esteem. Your self-esteem creates a mindset. You might know people with great financial wealth and maybe even a great physically fit body, yet they have zero relationships and are alone in the world. You might know someone who has great relationships and spends five hours at the gym every day, but they are broke. These are not examples of great self-esteem.

Be willing to examine your results. It takes a leader to sit down and be honest about their results. Ask yourself: what are my relationship results, what are my health and wellness results, what are my parenting results, what are my financial results, what are my making-a-difference results? These results are a reflection of your self-esteem. Change your results, change your self-esteem. Change your self-esteem, change your results.

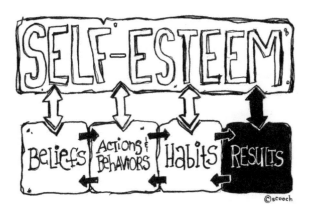

THE SMALL STUFF

Please note: The following lists are just examples to get you to identify some behaviors to support you on your journey. This is not an all-inclusive list, and you may come up with many additional items of your own.

Small actions that support a great relationship with a significant other:

1. Keeping your mouth shut when you want to criticize, complain, or be right.
2. Not always being right.
3. Apologizing often.
4. Celebrating significant other's occasions—birthdays, anniversaries, Mother's/Father's Day.
5. Making the time to take vacations and weekend trips.
6. Visiting the in-laws and their other family members.
7. Going to places your significant other likes that you don't like: museum, opera, baseball games.

8. Having family meetings.

9. Accepting responsibility for your choices.

10. Showing affection.

11. Taking an interest in your significant other's hobbies and interests.

12. Compromising on vacation spots, restaurants, purchases, and child rearing.

13. Spending below your means.

14. Complimenting and supporting your significant other.

15. Helping with cleaning and childcare.

16. Being passionate, fun, solution-oriented, loving, trusting, vulnerable, and positive.

17. Keeping your agreements.

Small actions that do not support a great relationship with a significant other:

1. Complaining, criticizing, and acting condescending.

2. Having contempt for your significant other.

3. Giving the silent treatment.

4. Sleeping on the couch.

5. Talking behind his/her back.

6. Withholding sex.

7. Watching TV in silence night after night.

8. Blaming and never accepting responsibility.

9. Blaming significant other or kids for your choices.

10. Always needing things your way.

11. Always needing to be right.

12. Not helping with cleaning, childcare, or other shared responsibilities.

13. Spending above your means.

14. Being distrustful, jealous, angry, negative, closed off, boring, or predictable.

15. Not keeping your agreements.

Small actions that support great relationships with children:

1. Reading books together.

2. Going to the games, recitals, and plays.

3. Eating dinner as a family.

4. Going on vacations and trips.

5. Keeping your agreements.

6. Playing games.

7. Having a good relationship with the other parent.

8. Giving them choices.

9. Being involved in education, friends, and activities.

10. Living your dreams, taking risks.

11. Disciplining, guiding, parenting.

12. Picking them up on time.

13. Showing affection.

14. Giving compliments and building them up.

15. Setting up boundaries and rules.

16. Being fun, passionate, spontaneous, loving, trusting, and unconditional.

17. Doing things your kids like that you don't like.

18. Wearing costumes.

Small actions that do not support great relationships with children:

1. Missing games, recitals, and plays.

2. Breaking your agreements.

3. Speaking poorly about the other parent.

4. Instilling a dictatorship.

5. Criticizing, calling names.

6. Yelling, screaming.

7. Not listening.

8. Having no boundaries, letting them do whatever they want.

9. Not spending time with them.

10. Lying.

11. Picking them up late.

12. Being boring, angry, distrustful, or closed off.

Small actions that support a great career:

1. Taking time to get educated, formal or not.

2. Keeping your agreements.

3. Being willing to spend extra time—coming in early, staying late.

4. Arriving on time.

5. Paperwork is accurate and timely.

6. Taking opportunities when presented.

7. Creating opportunities.

8. Being willing to make the scary phone calls.

9. Taking risks.

10. Going to classes, seminars, workshops, leadership training.

11. Being passionate, solution-oriented, positive, persistent, results-oriented, and loyal.

12. Being great at certain things.

13. Being known for something.

14. Being willing to go above and beyond.

15. Making the hard decisions.

Small actions that do not support a great career:

1. Being late for work, business meetings, or lunch.
2. Lying, stealing, cheating.
3. Not spending time on education or training.
4. Only being willing to work the hours paid for.
5. Complaining, criticizing.
6. Being average.
7. Being negative, boring, grumpy, complacent, or disloyal.
8. Not being great at any one thing.
9. Partying every night.
10. Paperwork inaccurate or late.
11. Taking versus adding value.
12. Having opinions and values that are easily influenced.
13. Consistently having reasons and excuses.
14. Taking lots of time off.

Small actions that support financial success:

1. Living beneath your means consistently.
2. Years of saving; starting to save small and soon.
3. Being financially educated by taking seminars and classes and reading books.
4. Being organized with your paperwork/filing system.
5. Paying bills on time.
6. Resisting doodads—the latest cars, boats, toys.
7. Being willing to do uncomfortable things like meeting with key advisors and planning.
8. Learning leverage.
9. Protecting your credit score.
10. Having multiple sources of income.

11. Looking for ways to keep more money

12. Having a spending plan.

Small actions that do not support financial success:

1. Years of living above your means.

2. Years of instant gratification.

3. Buying things to impress people.

4. Trading time for money.

5. Hoping to get rescued.

6. Buying doodads—the latest cars, watches, technology.

7. Staying financially uneducated.

8. Not having financial goals, not planning.

9. Being more committed to comfortable things like watching TV, eating out, taking time off.

10. Paying bills late.

11. Only having one source of income.

12. Not protecting your credit score.

13. Buying more house or car than you need or can afford.

14. Not having a spending plan.

15. Starting to save large and late.

16. Buying with credit things that depreciate.

17. Paying late charges and finance charges.

Small actions that support great health and wellness:

1. Years of consistent exercise.

2. Attending doctor and dentist appointments regularly.

3. Eating a good diet.

4. Drinking water.

5. Spending time meal prepping versus eating out.

6. Practicing moderation.

7. Becoming educated about nutrition, cholesterol, high blood pressure.

8. Flossing your teeth.

9. Getting up and going to the gym.

10. Maintaining good personal hygiene and grooming.

11. Doing things today to feel good tomorrow.

12. Taking the stairs.

13. Getting an adequate amount of sleep.

Small actions that do not support great health and wellness:

1. Sitting on the couch, watching TV.

2. Eating fast food.

3. Drinking too much alcohol or doing drugs.

4. Not taking necessary medication.

5. Missing doctor and dentist appointments.

6. Sleeping in versus going to the gym.

7. Ordering dessert regularly.

8. Consistently consuming more calories than you burn.

9. Feeling good in the moment.

10. Not drinking enough water.

11. Not getting enough sleep.

The best indicator for what the next 10 years of your life are going to look like is based on what you did (or didn't do) over the last 10 years. That means if you do nothing differently for the next 10 years, you shouldn't be surprised if your life doesn't change. Based on this concept, think about what your marriage will be like if you do nothing different for the next 10 years. What about your financial situation? What about the relationship with your kids? Your weight?

> "If you do not change direction, you may end up where you are heading."
> — LAO TZU —

Examining our results can be difficult—painful—and yet we must examine our results to establish our Point A: *where we are now.* Then, we must be willing to think differently. Act differently. Create new habits. Practice. As children, we were willing to practice over and over and over again. Remember, the best time to plant a tree is 20 years ago. The second best time is now.

No matter where you are or where you have been, you can go someplace different. That is the whole purpose of this book and what is so exciting.

No matter where you are right now, your life can look very different one year, five years, and especially 10 years from now. Regardless of what you have created, you can create something bigger and better. Yet, at this point, changing your future might look a little daunting. You have to remember to take it one day at time. That is how your current results were created. The next five chapters are designed to give you real-life tools, techniques, and strategies so you can create a personalized strategic plan.

> "When I lost all of my excuses, I found my results."
> — UNKNOWN —

PART 2

"Little is more impressive, inspirational, or sexy, than watching someone in the throes of action, driven by purpose, oblivious to all but their aim. Today has your name all over it."

- THE UNIVERSE -

CHAPTER 5
BRING 100% OF YOURSELF TO THE PARTY:
TAP INTO YOUR INNER FIVE-YEAR-OLD!

My five-year-old daughter brings 100% of herself to the party every day. Her self-esteem is completely intact. From the moment she gets up to the moment she goes to bed, she is seeking the maximum amount of adventure and experience possible. When it is time for bed, she becomes a master negotiator and avoider. She begs for five more minutes 10 different times, like her whole life depends on those few minutes. She wants to start chewing gum immediately after waking up at 7:00 a.m. She wants to play with Play-Doh at 7:01 a.m. She wants to do everything in her wonderful world as soon as she opens her eyes.

She has also fully embraced the question "Why?" I have not found good answers to why a five-year-old cannot chew gum at 7:00 a.m. or why she cannot play with Play-Doh at 7:01 a.m. or why you cannot start eating the food before you leave the grocery store or why we cannot have ice cream more often. I have found myself at a loss for good, sound logic for many of my rules.

I am starting to sense that I will learn many profound lessons through my daughter. Through her, I will question the rules and boundaries by which I live my life. She will show me where I have stopped appreciating the small stuff: spending the day at a water park, having a picnic, or watering the flowers.

She shows me, in my busyness, that we have time. She shows me how fabulous it is to be new to this planet. She shows me daily how wonderful my husband is, how amazing I am, and how extraordinary the world is.

Small children have big emotions. They do not hesitate to bring passion to pancakes for breakfast, playing, avoiding naps or bedtime, or any of the million small parts of their day.

JUMP OFF THE MERRY-GO-ROUND

What percentage of yourself are you currently bringing to the party? How much you bring to the party is in direct proportion to your level of self-esteem. Once again, imagine a meter that measures from 0 to 100, representing the possible percentage you are bringing to the party. Be honest. What is your number? What percentage of you are you bringing to your significant other? Your children? Your business?

Come up with one number. Is it 66%? Maybe 72% or 83%? Imagine if your number is 72%. If you are only bringing 72% of yourself to the party called life, then you are only getting back 72% of what is available. It is a universal law that what you put out into the world comes back in equal amounts. You put out 72%, you get back 72%.

Now, imagine that you decide to bring more of yourself to the party. You start bringing 90%. What could you be doing on Saturday nights at 90% that you aren't doing at 72%? How would your marriage be different? Your bank account? Think about this: When was the last time that you were willing to bring 100% of yourself to the party? One hundred percent. No holding back. For most people, the last time they brought 100% of themselves to the party was way back when they were five years old. That explains why so many people live their lives in a way that lacks passion and energy.

What percentage of yourself are you bringing to the party? ____%

Five-year-olds bring 100% of themselves to the party every day, all day, day after day after day. They don't go for two weeks and then require a day off. They don't know how to not bring 100%. And because they bring 100%, they have extraordinary relationships and results. They lead passionate lives.

Young children are completely open, honest, loving, and unconditional; hence, they experience genuine relationships with everyone. They have perfect self-expression. They have extraordinary self-esteem. You never have to wonder what a five-year-old is thinking or feeling; they express it.

And then they move on—they switch. They can be having a temper tantrum on the floor, experience it fully, and moments later be happily playing outside. And they are not outside holding onto a grudge, planning revenge on mom. They have moved on, fully intact.

What if you had perfect self-expression? What if the people in your life didn't have be mind readers with your thoughts and feelings? If you were as trusting, open, and as honest as a five-year-old, how would your relationships be different? What if you were able to switch your feelings, your mood, in moments versus days, weeks, months, or even years?

Five-year-olds are 100% committed to the end result, too. It could be a cookie or a new toy—it doesn't really matter. What's important is that, in the child's mind, failure is not an option! If mom says no, they go to dad. If dad says no, they go to grandma. If grandma says no, they get out a ladder or stepstool and go for the cookie themselves. And, while all this is going on, they are not concerned with what anyone thinks or who might get mad.

They are focused on the end result and their success. Most adults give up after their first "no." Most children take more risks in a day than the majority of adults take over the course of a whole year. Children are in action, failing forward, while a lot of adults are busy thinking about it, planning, getting ready to get ready, or already assuring themselves that their end result is either hopelessly out of reach or too stupid to reach for. Can you imagine a five-year-old leaving Toys "R" Us and asking for a brochure so he could think about his future purchase? Five-year-olds are riding an exciting, adventurous roller coaster, while the adults stay safe on the merry-go-round. This is true emotionally, as well.

Name a specific relationship that you could bring more of yourself to *today*: _____.

If you ask a five-year-old what they want, they have a list—usually a long list. They have clarity. When you ask an adult the same question, you usually get the answer, "I don't know." What if you had a vision, a crystal clear vision? What if you were willing to declare it? When a five-year-old wants something, they want it now. They are urgent about all things.

Do you know adults who live in some-a-day? Some-a-day when I get my degree, I can have the career I want. Some-a-day when my kids leave the house, I can think about me. We act like we have all the time in the world. You would not see a five-year-old deciding on a new toy and then scheduling delivery for nine months in the future. Five-year-olds live in the moment, squeezing every last drop out of every day. They are not concerned with what happened yesterday, not fearful of tomorrow.

"There are only 7 days in the week, and someday is not one of them."

- RITA CHAND -

Children are passionate, positive, and optimistic: they see the wonder in everything. Children are willing to access the full spectrum of their emotions, talents, and the skills that are available to them, while some adults remain fearful, cautious, and self-conscious. These adults run their whole lives by what other people think. You ask an adult, "How are you doing?" *Fine. Everything is fine.* Not too high, not too low, just right around the center line.

And when it comes to setbacks, children move on. Yes, they may cry at first, but they will quickly dry their tears and focus on the next thing. Some adults, unfortunately, have forgotten how to move on. They just continue to carry their burdens with them for years, refusing to let go and preventing themselves from moving onward to a better place.

LIFE IS NOT BORING

Five-year-olds are rarely bored. They play with pots and pans, they make mud pies, they create make-believe friends if needed. They are creative and imaginative. How many adults do you know who are bored with their jobs, their friendships, or their activities?

A friend of mine was at Disneyland with his daughter. He saw a man walking towards him with a t-shirt that said, "Life is not boring." Hmm, he thought. After the man had passed, my friend turned to look to see that the back of the t-shirt said, "You are."

Some of you have become quite boring. Predictable, even. I am guilty of this, as well.

Is it possible that the people in your life are screaming for something different? Give the people what they want! What they want is outrageous, spontaneous, fun, playful...different. What they want is anything other than normal.

Imagine what you normally do, how you normally do it, and then throw that out the window. It's boring. It's predictable. Stop being predictable. Do things that make their eyes bulge. Do things to make them feign embarrassment, though they are watching every moment. Be willing to put on costumes and makeup, go on bumper boats, join in skits, be silly, leave love notes, send them a not-perfect video, jump in a fountain. Be vulnerable. The key here is your willingness to not look good...or even look silly or awkward. Most people are so preoccupied with making sure they look good they are missing out on something huge.

> "In the willingness to look bad is when you look oh, so good."
> - RENEE CERMAK -

It is in the willingness to look bad that you oftentimes gain the respect of the entire room. My husband and I love the Broadway show *Mamma Mia*. We see it quite often. Over the years, with some help from my family, my husband decided that "Dancing Queen" was my theme song. Every time it came on he would say, "It's your theme song."

Five years ago, I threw my husband an over-the-top 50th birthday party. I decided I would surprise my husband and perform "Dancing Queen"—the way they do at the end of *Mamma Mia*, when the three women come out in orange, pink, and green costumes from a 70s rock band and perform "Dancing Queen." I enrolled my sister and a friend to join me. I had my friend sew elaborate costumes. We had wardrobe fittings, practiced, and perfected our moves. I would not say we "nailed it," but I completed my mission.

A couple of days later, I went to meet with the photographer to look at the photos from the party. Flipping through the photographs, the photographer stopped on one photograph of my husband and said, "That's why you did it, right? For that look right there." It was a picture of my husband watching my "Dancing Queen" performance—eyes bulging, jaw dropped, and the biggest grin on his face. I, too, can appear boring and predictable to my husband but not that night.

BE THE FUN, BRING THE FUN

Think back to when you were younger and you couldn't stand the thought of missing a second of the action. If it was time for you to go to bed but your parents or siblings were still awake, it may have been impossible for you to fall asleep—you didn't want to miss a moment! The last thing a five-year-old wants to do is take a nap, yet a nap is usually at the top of an adult's want list.

If you were at the beach, that's where you were! The sand and ocean were your focus—nothing else mattered. You weren't making sure sand did not get on your beach towel. You weren't worried about what the sun's rays were doing.

What if you allowed yourself to have more fun? What if you taught yourself how to create more fun? Five-year-olds create fun wherever they go; they don't wait for it to happen. There are many adults who reserve all of their fun for an entire year and then expend it in two weeks of vacation. Children would never do this.

There are people who spend more time planning for their vacations than they plan for their life, their vision, their retirement, and their legacy. What if you spent more time incorporating fun in the other 50 weeks of the year? Having and/or creating fun anywhere, anytime, no matter what is happening is a skill. It's also a habit; just like being boring is a habit. For a five-year-old, having fun is a priority, a focus. Very much like my sister, Robin. She is a great example of having a commitment to fun. If you want her to do something, her first question will be, "Is it going to be fun?"

My family is known for bringing more fun to everything they do. Last month, three of my sisters and my brother were driving to a funeral for a close family friend in Pittsburgh. About halfway through the five-hour drive, they started harassing me with texts to amuse themselves.

First, they told me that they would not pass on my condolences unless I played with them. Among their offers they asked if I would like to sponsor their next road trip convenience store stop. It would allow me to be part of the trip in spirit, they said. *Yes, of course, why would I not want to do that? What a great offer.* So they bought lottery tickets, beef jerky, Swedish fish, a balloon animal maker, a big box of jokes, Pringles, M&Ms, Mentos, and Chex Mix, all for $48. They were happy for hours, especially because they didn't pay.

CERMAK FAMILY TIPS TO BRING MORE FUN TO EVERYTHING YOU DO:

If you are going to do it, get all of your friends involved.

Make sure there is a theme.

Keep dice in your purse. You never know when you will have 15 minutes for a game of Farkle.

Put time limits on anything: making lunch, playing a game, going in the grocery store. Urgency makes everything more fun.

When possible, use other people's money.

When in doubt, have a scavenger hunt.

Move aside, we are the fun.

When possible, include strangers.

Do not be normal.

Anybody can sing and dance, especially with a group behind them.

Be abundant with the use of costumes.

You can celebrate anything; celebrations are often how memories are made.

Divide the overwhelming into manageable pieces. My brother and sisters used to divide cleaning the kitchen into over 50 tasks. Then we would pick tasks out of a hat. Yes, our way took longer, but it was more fun!

What if you could master having fun anywhere, anytime, no matter what is happening? The more passion you can bring to the mundane, the easier it will be for you to embrace your goals when they manifest in your life. Paradoxically, you need to live with passion so that the things you are truly passionate about can make an appearance in your life.

❝ Support passions in anyone, no matter how strange or small. When my son Otto was four, he wanted to open a worm stand (like people would do with lemonade) because he loved worms. We spent a hot summer day building and painting the worm stand, and then 'opened' for business the next day. I really didn't expect that we would sell a single worm, but who am I to squash his ideas? And the process of painting the signs and making the booth was fun in itself.

Clearly, other people have similar ideas because a man pulled up and said, 'Worms? Worms? Well, I'll take all the worms ya got!' We had 19. We sold out in the first hour and that man is now a great friend of ours.

There was a sign on the side of the road advertising the worm stand, 'Brinklow Brothers Home of the Lucky Worm.' That sign hung there for two years. One day, we were in line at Safeway and Otto, who was five at that time, wanted a DVD. I told him he could buy it, but it would cost him 50 worms (10 cents a piece is what they sold for). His eyes opened real big and he put it back. Then he tried something else that was 30 worms, and then he settled on a '10 worm' yogurt. The guy behind us in line looked at me funny, so I said, 'Oh, they own a worm business, so it is helpful for him to understand how much work he would have to do in order to get the item.' The man looked at us and said, 'Are these the Brinklow Brothers?' Safeway was at least a 10-minute drive from our house. The worm stand remained in business for two years with a total of 5,000 worms sold. **❞**

- Erin Cermak

Why did people buy 5,000 worms? Because worms are great for composting. They take your food waste and turn it into rich, dark, crumbly dirt for your garden. Of course, Erin taught her two sons marketing, so they created "Peace, Love & Worms" t-shirts to sell. I own a couple. They even had an online store. My sister tells me they made $1,000, which they invested, and today has grown to $2,000.

This concept may be obvious by this point, but the moment

you minimize the importance of the small stuff, you will begin to decrease your chances for success. Without conscious awareness of the importance of the little things, it's easy to forget about pushing yourself to do the little things consistently. That is when you may fall back into the mindset that the majority of people hold: that only the big things matter. But it's the small moments that build a great life, not just the momentous occasions.

What if you could bring passion to the everyday, to the daily grind—like a five-year-old? Have you seen a five-year-old brush her teeth? Mundane and boring? No; usually it's a creative mess. And yet it is an everyday activity. There is nothing momentous about it. Not surprisingly, the daily grind factors into your overall results more than the momentous days. So, don't discount the importance of what you do on a daily basis, no matter how unimportant or mundane certain actions may appear to you. Instead, act more like a five-year-old and bring *passion* to it.

The great news is that we were all were five years old at one time, and we can reclaim our passion. At some point in our lives, no matter how long ago, we all brought 100% of ourselves to the party, and 100% of our self-esteem was intact.

If we are as open, honest, and unconditional now as we were then, we can have better relationships. Or if someone hurts us, we can forge ahead into new relationships without being overly guarded and fearful. If we go after our financial goals the same way a five-year-old goes after a coveted toy, we will definitely have more money! And if we allow our imaginations to soar like that of a small child, we will reignite our passion for living and truly believe that our dreams are possible to achieve.

> "Every child is an artist. The problem is how to remain an artist once he grows up."
>
> - PABLO PICASSO -

CHAPTER 6
BEING SELFISH IS A GOOD THING!

One of my boyfriends broke my heart and then married a friend of mine. At the time, I viewed this as the ultimate betrayal, punishable by evil thoughts and eternal silence. For a while, I gathered my supporters, displayed my evidence, got my sympathy, justified my stance, replayed my story (yes, it is called being a victim), and chipped away at my self-esteem. Then, my best friend invited a group of people, including the three of us, on a very important birthday cruise.

I had two options. Option #1: continue the silence and make the entire group miserable and probably behave in ways that I would regret later. Option #2: take the high road; open communication (actually speak to "them"), have fun with "them," forgive "them," and positively contribute to my friend's birthday celebration.

I am grateful to have been forced into the "opportunity" and even more grateful that I chose option #2. I was able to change my view, my perception, and how I wanted to *be* moving forward. I have thanked myself countless times for taking the high road on that cruise and for making my self-esteem the top priority. However, I did it for me, not for them. I know *that* switch in my thinking and behavior contributed to meeting my husband one month later.

My husband and I have continued our relationship with this couple for years, bonding over dinners, conferences, and even vacations. Every time I see them, I think about the choices I made that led us to this moment. If I had chosen to be "right," continued my silence, and refused to forgive, things could be very different for me. And my self-esteem smiles. Every time. Everyone wins because I chose to forgive first for *my* benefit, not theirs. Every time I see them or even think about how I handled the situation, I get a boost in my self-esteem.

The opposite would be true had I chosen not to forgive. Every time I would have seen them or thought about how I had handled the situation, it would have chipped away at my self-esteem. I would have an example of myself being petty, stubborn, angry, and a victim. I would have had to look at the fact that I had the opportunity to be the bigger person, and I blew it.

GIVE YOURSELF SOMEBODY TO LIKE

You have to make your self-esteem your #1 priority. Increasing your self-esteem is about bringing the biggest and best you to all areas of your life. When you bring the biggest and best you to the world, everybody wins: your significant other, your kids, your business, and every relationship in your life.

- When you have better health and live longer, your family wins.
- When you take a stand and set boundaries, your kids win.
- When you make more money and tithe 10%, your community wins.

When you are on an airplane with a child, the flight attendant is required to tell you that in case of emergency, you must put your oxygen mask on first before you assist your child. Why? Because if *you* do not get the oxygen mask on, how can you help your child? Can you see the parallel for other situations in life, such as moving forward after your divorce, getting your financial house in order, or eating healthy? Making your self-esteem a priority allows your children to get the best version of you.

Remember, self-esteem means your self-estimate, which means that for everyone to win, *you must put your self-esteem first.* In a way, you must be "selfish." You must make your self-esteem your #1 priority—a place where you actively play, create, and strategize. It is a guarantee that your self-esteem will be right by your side for the rest of your life. It is not a guarantee that anyone else will be. It is you and your self-esteem until the end.

I like to think of me and my self-esteem skipping down the beach, hand in hand, music playing, wind blowing—yes, like a Viagra commercial. What about my husband? He is the lucky one that gets to spend time with "us" a couple hours each day.

You invest time and money in your relationship with your significant other, your kids, your pets, and even your car. Just like those relationships, your self-esteem requires careful attention and nurturing. This is the most important relationship, as it is the driver of all other relationships.

Perhaps a close friend calls you, asking for help with packing for her upcoming move. Why do that favor for your friend? *Because it will increase your self-esteem.*

Or you feel like your wife is picking a fight with you, just waiting for you to take the bait and argue back. Why stay neutral? *Because it will increase your self-esteem.* Participating in the argument will decrease your self-esteem.

Your best friend betrays you. Why forgive? *Because it will increase your self-esteem.* Not forgiving and holding on to resentments, or acting out in revenge, will decrease your self-esteem.

You forgive for you, not for them. When you forgive, you get to move forward and give to a new, worthy best friend. It doesn't mean you condone their behavior or that there will still be a relationship, it means that you are not leaving behind any of your energy or power.

In the same vein, start doing things for the simple reason that your *inaction* will *decrease* your self-esteem. For instance, let's say you promised your friend that you would attend his business presentation. When the time comes, the presentation is inconvenient and you don't feel like going. Sure, you could stay home, watch TV, and take a nap. But don't take the easy way out. Get up and go! Why?

In this case, you're not going for your friend's benefit, you are going because keeping your word will increase your self-esteem. Most importantly, you are going because *not* keeping your word will decrease your self-esteem. So, instead of looking at it as an inconvenient obligation, maybe you could change your view to that of an opportunity to raise your own self-esteem. When you are willing to change your view, a whole new world opens up. What else might fall in the category of self-esteem opportunities masked by inconvenient obligations?

- Attending a baby shower, birthday party, or wedding.
- Stopping to help someone fix a flat tire.
- Contributing manual labor to a community service project.
- Babysitting your friend's baby.
- Calling your mother.
- Spending 15 minutes talking to your elderly neighbor.
- Sending a birthday card in the mail.

PROTECT YOUR SELF-ESTEEM

In situations where you have already given your word, you want to follow through. In the process, you may discover that you want to be more careful with what you give your word to. When you realize that your self-esteem is directly tied to how often you keep your word, you may also realize that it is okay to say no. In fact, it is very important for you to say no.

People with high self-esteem say "no" more often than they say "yes." When you say yes to one thing, it means you have to say no to other things. If I say yes to five speaking engagements this month, I am also saying no to spending those nights with my husband and daughter. For every yes, there is a price. Weigh them out. If the price is too high, say no.

There is another reason that people with high self-esteem say no more often than they say yes: because they realize that when they say yes to someone or something, it means that their name is on it. If their name is on it, failure is not an option.

Two years ago, I was facilitating a 90-day course for achieving goals. It was also a "90-day let's see what you are made of" and a "90-day play the biggest game of your life" course. All participants were told to set goals that were important to them, to set goals around things they had always wanted to do, and to set goals with a compelling *why* behind them.

One of the women in the course set a goal of taking 26 pole-dancing lessons in 90 days. Her compelling *why* was that she wanted to reconnect with her femininity. I love that. About 60 days into the program, she was very behind on the goal and decided she was going to change it. Have you ever done this? She was openly telling other people that she had no intention of completing *this* goal. So I called her.

With attitude, she explained to me that the goal was stupid, she had no desire to learn *this form of exercise*, and that she would be taking no further action. Keep in mind that this woman was told to set goals that were important to *her* and to choose something she had *always wanted to do*.

I said, "I am sorry you set a stupid goal. I am sorry you don't have time. I am sorry you do not see the value in continuing. Quite honestly, I don't care how you feel about your goal. You can like it; you can hate it. You can have a great time or suffer through it: your choice. The only thing I care about is this: *your name is on it*. You might not currently care that your name is on it, but *I* do. So, what's the plan to get this goal done? Failure is not an option. Not reaching the goal will chip away at your self-esteem, and that can't happen." Realizing her self-esteem was on the line, she did what it took to complete the goal.

What if your reputation was this: *From small things to big things, if my name is on it, consider it a done deal.* You can take it to the bank. In order to achieve that, what would you need to stop putting your name on? Self-esteem chippers. Those times that you make an agreement that you have no intention of keeping.

If you knew that what you gave your word to was a done deal, what would you start giving your word to? Self-esteem boosters.

Doing what you say you are going to do is much bigger than an action: it's a mindset. And it's a rewarding mindset.

> "Do what you say you're going to do.
> Eventually, people start believing in you."
>
> - CHRIS GUILLEBEAU -

Using your self-esteem as the #1 consideration, where do you need to practice saying no? Where do you need to practice saying yes?

Where I need to practice saying no: _____

_____

Where I need to practice saying yes:_____
_____

You are always teaching people how to treat you and how to talk to you by what you allow. Be willing to take a stand for your self-esteem. You are the only gatekeeper to your self-esteem empire; you must guard it fiercely. You must be relentless about keeping it safe. Be discriminating about who you let in. It's important to say no to people that make a sport of tearing down your self-esteem. There are seven billion people in this world. You can afford to choose wisely.

> "No one can make you feel inferior without your consent."
> - ELEANOR ROOSEVELT -

I recall an Oprah Winfrey interview with Maya Angelou. Maya Angelou said that thoughts are things, and they stick to the wall. She said that she does not allow negativity in her house because, if she does, it will stick somewhere and stay in her house. If someone is gossiping in her house, she tells them, "Stop it, stop *it*. Not in my house."

She told a story of her and a man she was living with. She came downstairs, ready for a date, wearing a blue dress. He looked at her and said, "You should wear the red dress. You look better in the red one." She said she had his bags packed and on the curb that night. "That was one peck. If I allowed him to peck me that one time, he would have pecked me to death." The pecks remind me of the self-esteem chippers.

Another way to protect your self-esteem is to realize that what you surround yourself with is very important. What you surround yourself with is a direct reflection of your self-esteem. I am talking about the people you surround yourself with, the house or apartment you live in, the car you drive, and the clothes you wear.

Driving an unreliable car is a direct reflection of your self-esteem. Every time you get in that car, five times a day, your self-esteem takes a hit. I am not saying the car you drive is important because of what other people might think. It's not about what kind of car you drive; it's about how you *feel* or what you *think* when you get in the car you drive—how it affects your self-esteem.

It's not about what kind of house you have; it's about how you *feel* or what you *think* every time you step in your door—how it affects your self-esteem. It's not about the clothes you wear; it's about how they affect your self-esteem.

What you surround yourself with creates your environment. What if you gave yourself an environment that increased your self-esteem at every turn; every time you got dressed, walked in your house, sat in your car, or looked around at your friends?

❝ I style people. They come to me for help with outfits, to show them how to put together items they already own, to add items to their wardrobe, or dress for a special event. Most of the time, I am just helping someone develop a signature style or look.

But sometimes, there are people who, in the beginning, seem to be all about the clothes and shoes, but half-way into the process the real issue comes up: it is their self-esteem, or lack of self-esteem. People spend lots of time hiding perceived flaws on their bodies. When they shop, they are shopping to hide. When they pick an outfit and get dressed, they are dressing to not get noticed. Typically, it's women. They stand in their closets looking over their clothes for hours before they put something on or they wear the same things they always wear because they are just comfortable enough in it and don't have to think about their clothes or their appearance when they are carrying on with their day. Here is what I have learned by helping people with their image: when a person thinks they look good, they feel good. When they feel good, they show confidence. When they are confident, their self-esteem raises through the roof. When people look good and feel good about how they are dressed they do different things. They stand taller, walk prouder, smile more and take more risks; they are willing to be noticed.

I remember one woman who had just lost over 65 pounds. She was a short woman with a thin frame and, when I met her, I never would have guessed she had previously carried a lot of extra weight on her currently skinny body. But she had several areas of very loose skin—belly, backside, and thighs. This was really messing with her perception of her weight loss. She had accomplished something most people try and try to do but never succeed and she couldn't celebrate it because she was still dressing like a person hiding in her clothes so no one would see her. By the time I was done with her, she was wearing skin-tight dresses, skinny jeans, and even sleeveless, arm-baring tops. These are all things that she would have never done, even in her skinny body, because her self-esteem kept her thinking she was just too flabby still to wear the clothes she had always dreamed of wearing prior to losing the weight. In that one day, during the time we were together, just by showing her how to focus on accentuating her assets and positives, and how to put outfits together, her self-esteem shot through the roof. It was quite a transformation, and it was all in how she was looking at herself. She was the same person on the outside who walked in the door trying to hide and mask flaws, but now her self-esteem was soaring and she was ready to be noticed. **"**

\- Nicole Thompson

SELF-ESTEEM SECRET WEAPONS

If you want to increase the amount you like yourself, focusing on three secret weapons will give you the most bang for your buck. The first secret weapon is taking the high road. Anytime you are able to take the high road, you will add to your self-esteem.

What is the *high road?* It's taking a course of action that is honorable, dignified, or respected. It's taking the most positive, diplomatic, or ethical course. It is also choosing to not take the low road.

What is the *low road?* Taking a course of action which is disrespectful, negative, or unethical. When you take the low road, you blame, gossip, lie, and make people wrong. Every time you take the low road, you decrease your self-esteem. Every time you take the high road, you increase your self-esteem and your honor, dignity, and respect. Taking the high road can look many different ways:

- You have the opportunity to be right and make someone else wrong and you stay silent.
- Apologizing first.
- You have the opportunity for revenge and you turn away.
- You have the opportunity to alienate and you include.
- You're honest, even when it's not popular.
- You choose not to participate in the gossip, even when it's about someone you dislike.
- You take responsibility for your part when everyone else is blaming.

Most of the time, the only person who knows you took the high road is you. This is one of the reasons why it is so powerful! There is something magical about having positive secrets with yourself and the Universe. There is something about no one else knowing that can put a spring in your step.

The high road is not a popular road; it's wide open, practically empty. All the more reason to spend time there. The low road is very crowded. Taking the high road is also beneficial because it separates you from the masses.

There are people out there that have no idea that the high road is an option. There are other people who know about it, yet realize that the low road is easier. Separating yourself from the masses is a great way to increase your self-esteem, especially when you are listening to, and following, your own values and principles.

Every time you take the high road, you are not biting your tongue, apologizing, including, or forgiving *for the other person*. Instead, you're doing it *for you*. You are taking these actions to increase your self-esteem, not theirs. Of course, the friend, significant other, and the child may be grateful and may benefit, but the important point is that you are moving towards feeling better about you.

In this case, it's not about everyone else. It's all about you—and when you act in this way, you'll find that this is a *healthy* type of selfishness. Ironically, it could be construed as *selflessness* by others. You know the truth, and you know the win-win results that such "selfish" behavior imparts.

The second secret weapon to building self-esteem involves giving, contributing, and making a difference. By now, you know that I am a woman on a mission regarding self-esteem being your #1 priority. I am also a woman on a mission to get more people to see the value of giving their time, treasure (money), and talent (skills). Specifically, I am talking about tithing: giving away 10% of your income to places that feed you, teach you, or inspire you. Why? Because tithing is the ultimate secret weapon when it comes to increasing self-esteem. It's also a wealth-building secret.

"Tithing is the best-kept abundance and prosperity secret in existence. It's an old secret that works—yet has been virtually forgotten, never learned, or rarely tested. And it's a sensitive subject. Ask most people about their giving, and you'll likely hit a "hot button," as money is one of the last taboos. When you tithe, you experience a positive difference in your life. When you tithe, you're demonstrating an understanding of spiritual truths and the Universal Laws."

- MARK VICTOR HANSEN -

I grew up with a very limited view regarding giving money (tithing). In my house, tithing meant giving 10% to the Catholic Church. It was something I was told to do, versus understanding the value of doing so. I watched my mother put her envelope in the basket week after week, year after year, not even recognizing her perfect example of tithing, of consistently giving 10% of my parent's income. She was a huge part of my dad's ability to build wealth, and he probably never knew it.

Regardless, in my twenties, I was an inward focused and selfish adult. I did not give my money. I did not give my time. I did not give my talent. That is what happens when you live at 30 on the self-esteem meter. It takes a certain level of self-esteem to be able to give, then an even higher level to realize that giving, making a difference, and contributing is what life is all about. Some people spend the first half of their lives inward focused and "getting" (acquiring stuff) and then the second half giving it away and making a difference.

> "I believe we are each coded in our DNA to give. The more you give, the more fully you live. Every individual's purpose in tithing is to open up his/her awareness of spiritual truths and Universal Laws. Tithing helps you to truly know yourself. Tithing is essential to the development of the soul. In fact, I believe you can look at your giving in your checkbook, and it is a great barometer of your soul's development, evolution and growth."
>
> - MARK VICTOR HANSEN -

A number of years ago, I was asked to give a talk on giving and the value of tithing. My first thought, of course, was, "Who am I to give a talk on tithing?" Then I thought that maybe I am the perfect person, because I grew from a person who went from tithing 0% and seeing zero value in tithing, to a person who tithes 10% consistently.

I remember the first time I signed up for monthly auto-tithing to a nonprofit organization in 1999 (they charged $500 to my credit card every month). I thought, "Wow, that's $6,000...can I give away $6,000?" I remember signing the credit card slip. It was a pivotal moment in my giving career. Since then, my thinking about tithing has evolved.

My viewpoint now is that tithing 10% is a law that you don't mess with. It's a universal law! It's a spiritual law! And the rewards are too good! The rewards are for those to whom you give, but also to yourself via your self-esteem. Giving is a powerful self-esteem builder.

In the world of tithing, there are no rules. Make your own rules. Make a giving plan that works for you. Start somewhere. Do you want to give your time, your money, your talent (skills), or all three? Tithe to whatever organizations or causes speak to you.

It might be your church and where you gain spiritual wisdom, and it might be for animals, autism, breast cancer, battered women, the environment, homelessness, clean water, politics, or world peace. You might have organizations you support consistently through auto-tithing and organizations to which you make a one-time donation. If you are not able to tithe 10%, then start with 2% or 5%. Make it easy to give. Set up a tithing account (another savings account). When income comes in, immediately move 10% into your tithing account. That way, the money is there, ready and waiting. It is not painful when you make a donation, because you have already parted with the money.

"If we don't tithe, it means we are ignorant of the law of tithing, we don't believe in God's law, or we don't believe in the universal laws on which our planet relies. If you know you should tithe and don't, you will reap in experience what you sow in consciousness. It is not a punishment, it is simply the law. When you close up, the world closes up around you. If you show me a person having financial difficulties, I'll show you a non-tither or a tither with a bad attitude!

- MARK VICTOR HANSEN -

❝ Tithing has always been something in my heart that has felt right. However, after years of poor financial decisions and the crashing of the real estate market, tithing was the last thing my husband and I were thinking about. Our minds shifted into great scarcity as we found ourselves foreclosing on one investment property and doing a short sale on another. We had used up all our savings in an attempt to keep our rental properties afloat, and there was a day where my husband and I found ourselves in the parking lot of a grocery store crying because we had no idea how we were going to buy groceries for our four children.

We both committed to making drastic changes in our lives in order to bounce back from that time. It took us several years to dig ourselves out of that mess. During that time, I was reintroduced to the power of tithing, and decided that even though our get-out-of-debt plan did not originally include tithing, I decided to start. At that time, I had a financial goal to create $50,000 in 90 days. It was more money than I had ever made in that amount of time. I knew I had to make drastic changes to my daily habits in order to achieve this.

With my first check, I started my tithing. It was the largest amount I had ever tithed and, even though my scarcity mentality was screaming in my head, I went ahead and dropped the check off at my church. I continued to tithe with each check I received. At the 45-day mark, I was a little over $7,000 short of being 50% on track. I had no idea how I would be able to reach this, and then I received a visitor at my office. He was a commercial real estate agent that I had referred a client to almost two years prior. I had actually forgotten I had given him this referral. He came with great news that they finally closed on their transaction that morning, and my referral fee was $7,400. WHAT?! It was exactly what I needed to be on track with my goal. It was a game changer for me that day. Of course, it is not every day that I am getting news of a $7,400 referral fee, however, amazing things have happened in my life by choosing to make tithing a part of my life plan. **❞**

- Jessica Morel

©scooch

The third secret weapon in building high self-esteem is the abnormal and uncommon action of taking responsibility for your choices, actions, behaviors, and results. Inherent in taking responsibility is giving up blame, justifications, excuses, and *victim consciousness*.

When you live from victim consciousness, it means that things happen to you. That you and your results are at the whims of other people, the weather, or other uncontrollable events—outside circumstances. You do not have control; other people or things control what happens *to* you. And there is nothing you can do about it. The world is full of victims; they are everywhere. Turn on the TV, read the newspapers, and listen to your coworkers. In current society, it is okay to be a victim; it is normal to be a victim; it is often even rewarded to be a victim.

Yet the more of a victim you are, the less self-esteem you have. You can be a victim or you can have high self-esteem, not both.

We are victim to people: significant others, children, bosses, employees, business owners, parents.

My boyfriend is the reason this relationship is not working. If he would only change, then...

I should have been promoted by now. I am smarter and faster. My supervisor is jealous of my skills and has found ways to hold me back.

The babysitter was late.

We are victim to groups of people: the government, politicians, lawyers, ethnic groups.

I don't have work because there are too many illegal immigrants.

Clearly the government is to blame. My taxes are so high, I will never be wealthy.

We are victim to circumstances.

Well, I would have been on time if it wasn't for the rain or the snow or the traffic or the flat tire.

Boss, we did not meet the deadline for the project because of the manufacturer, or we didn't have enough time, or because of the new budget.

There is always a reason or excuse. It's somebody else's fault. Victims often say things like, "It wasn't my fault," or "There was nothing I could do," or "They made me," or "I had no choice."

Being a victim is associated with being powerless, helpless, not in control, or hurt. So, why would we do this? The only reason why we do anything—*there are benefits.* We get to avoid, blame, and justify. We get to avoid facing the truth about ourselves. As victims, we get sympathy, attention, even money. We get to control and manipulate others. As victims, we don't have to change, and we have good reasons for not being extraordinary. You are not able to be a victim and be extraordinary because you are powerless and not in control.

"If you habitually react or respond to circumstances, where does the power lie in these situations? It clearly lies outside you, in the circumstances. Therefore, because the power does not reside in you, you are powerless and the circumstances are all-powerful."

- ROBERT FRITZ -

The opposite of being a victim is to take responsibility, to stop blaming, and to look in the mirror and ask, "How did I create this? What is my responsibility in this result? What are the choices that I made or didn't make? What are the actions that I took or didn't take? What are the things I said or didn't say that caused this result?"

This is a switch from allowing things to happen *to* you, to *making* things happen. You are responsible for your choices, your actions, and your results—good or bad, effective or ineffective. The more responsibility you are willing to take, the higher your self-esteem will be because, when you take responsibility, you experience power, freedom, and being in control.

Victim and *responsible* are different perspectives delivering different amounts of self-esteem and very different results. It's not that being a victim is bad and being responsible is good; they are two different ways to experience life. When you choose *victim*, you choose a certain experience. When you choose *responsible*, you choose a very different experience. It is very normal to be victim to circumstances. It's what most people do. The problem is that with this choice, you'll get the results that most people get, and you have to give up high self-esteem.

Taking responsibility is very abnormal and uncommon. People will notice because it is so strange to not blame. When you take responsibility, you separate yourself from the masses of normal, common, and average. The more you like yourself, the easier it is to take responsibility. The more you like yourself, the easier it is to stick out in the crowd. At some point, if you keep increasing the amount you like yourself, going victim to outside circumstances is no longer an option because you are a superhero. What if your superpower was taking personal responsibility?

REPLAY

There are certain events or experiences (both good and bad) that I call *the 100 replay videos*—moments we remember and replay. It could be an embarrassing moment, a proud moment, or a situation you handled poorly or masterfully. These are the moments that we replay in our minds over and over and over. If we deem them bad, every time we hit the replay button we are chipping at our self-esteem. Remember: these can be good, too.

When you forgive a friend who has betrayed you and then move on, you've created a video worth replaying. And maybe every time you see her, you hit the replay button on how you handled that situation and you increase your self-esteem. Think about your most embarrassing moment. How many times have you replayed the video of what you did or said? How many times since it happened has it chipped at your self-esteem? Now think about your proudest moment, you in all your glory. How many times have you replayed that video, increasing your self-esteem?

How you end relationships—all relationships—can be a big contributor to your "replay videos," hence your self-esteem. What you say, what you do, and how you act can haunt you for years or build you up. And "what goes around comes around."

How you end relationships also determines how you move forward, meaning your energy level, attitude, participation level, and future outlook. You can move forward happy or angry, responsible or blaming, with integrity or without integrity. How you move forward affects your self-esteem and your future relationships.

You have heard the phrase, "Don't burn bridges." I have an expectation that any relationship that ends will very likely resurface at some point—maybe once, maybe repeatedly for life. The next time I see them, I want my self-esteem to be happy about how I handled it. This expectation causes me to think differently, behave differently, and act differently during the breakup.

I often remind myself that this person might have one of the keys to my success 10 years from now, or I might need them to give me a job or a recommendation in the future. Ex-boyfriends included. If they had enough good qualities for me to spend a couple of years with them, then they have enough good qualities for me to be friends with them. Plus, they can give me invaluable advice, because they know me.

I remember one ex-boyfriend who said that he was never going to talk to me again, and I said, "*Yes, you are!* We are going to be friends someday!" And we are. Every time I see him and his family, my self-esteem smiles. And, of course, the Universe tested my commitment to stay friendly with ex-boyfriends, as seen in my high road example at the beginning of the chapter. The Universe will test your commitments, every time, for your benefit.

I am including this next section as a Public Service Tip. I would not recommend having an affair while you are in a committed relationship. Cheating, being unfaithful, adulterous, untrue, disloyal, traitorous, two-faced, false, double-crossing, and deceitful—all are words that you do not want associated with your self-esteem.

Clearly, being unfaithful is not good from a moral standpoint—it's one of the Ten Commandments. However, when you look at it from a self-esteem and a *100 replay* perspective, it might be worse. When you cheat on a diet, you may remember it for a couple months, maybe even years. When you cheat on a test, eventually you will let it go. Cheating on a significant other, in my non-experiential opinion, stays with you for life.

Every time the subject of being unfaithful is brought up, you will connect to it and replay your videos, even if you are in a different marriage. It sticks with you, it sticks *to* you, like Maya Angelou said. And every time you think about you being unfaithful and untrue, you will peck and chip at your self-esteem.

On the days that your limiting beliefs are looking for evidence of why you are untrustworthy, deceitful, and disloyal they will remind you of the affair over and over. Here is the Public Service Tip: please do not have an affair; it is a top-five self-esteem killer. You can see that I am speaking from a self-esteem perspective, not a moral perspective. Clearly, moral reasons are often not enough.

What if you strategically gave yourself more positive replay videos and fewer negative ones? What if you didn't wait for the positive ones to happen, you created them? What if you didn't wait for the negative ones to happen, you avoided them? If the self-chipping video has already been recorded, when it plays you can stop it in its tracks.

You can positively interfere with the replay by immediately doing something else: pushups, looking at an award, replaying your proudest moment, or calling someone and asking them to tell you how great you are. What if you lived by the question: If I do X, will it increase or decrease my self-esteem? And let the answer make your decision. It is smart to say no if what you are going to do will result in decreasing your self-esteem—purposefully hurting someone else, lying, stealing, or cheating. Play out the video in advance. Choose wisely.

Before you do anything, consider your self-esteem first.

Giving yourself someone to like may be a revolutionary concept, but consider the ramifications of living life in a new way: what if you gave *yourself* somebody to be proud of? Someone to root for? Someone to respect? What if you were your biggest fan? Would you agree that you are going to judge yourself for the rest of your life? Nicely or harshly? Would you agree that you are your own biggest critic? Give your judge, give your critic, someone to like.

> "Ever loved someone so much, you would do anything for them? Yeah, well, make that someone yourself and do whatever the hell you want."
>
> - HARVEY SPECTER -

What actions could you take to like yourself? Give three compliments per day. Arrive to work five minutes early. Leave love notes in your child's lunch. Participate in community service. Tip 25%. Do more than your share. Create positive habits. Be helpful.

Create a list of 5 actions you will take to like yourself.

1. _____

2. _____

3. _____

4. _____

5. _____

Give your judge/critic someone to be proud of. *What actions could you take to be proud of yourself?* Consistently work out at 5:00 a.m. Raise $5,000 for charity. Learn a language. Spend quality time with your children. Accomplish goals. Rescue an animal.

Create a list of 5 actions you will take to be proud of yourself.

1. _____
2. _____
3. _____
4. _____
5. _____

Give yourself someone to respect. *What actions could you take to respect yourself?* Ask for a promotion. Learn new skills. Share your expertise. Take a stand. Say no to your child. Take care of your body. Dress well. Create boundaries.

Create a list of 5 actions you will take to respect yourself.

1. _____
2. _____
3. _____
4. _____
5. _____

If you start acting with the intention of *increasing* your self-esteem, you'll find that putting yourself first, considering your self-esteem first, pays big dividends—to you AND to everyone else. Since your vote is the only vote that matters in the end, it has to be the #1 priority. No excuses!

CHAPTER 7
GOAL SETTING VERSUS GOAL ACHIEVING

" IT WAS AMAZING! It was the first two feet that were the most difficult—it was like Renee talking about being in that scary zone and running back to comfort. Not only did I stand on the bottom to see the surface looking up—45 feet up—and saw the most amazing colors and a whole new world of beauty, I was so **PROUD** of myself for not giving up, for breaking through my limiting beliefs, and taking a risk.

I learned a lot from this dive. I realized how I do this with almost every area in my life. I start a new challenge, get so excited about it, then get out of my safety zone, and want to give up. I even set myself up for failure by **NOT PREPARING!** Seriously, how many opportunities did I have to get my certification prior to going! I even gave up my first try—I totally freaked out! The coolest part was that I was able to recognize my thinking and what was holding me back.

I noticed how quick I was to justify giving up (not being ready...), and then how much the disappointment would chip away at me. There have been several goals over my life that I have set and not followed through with. I am one Spanish class away from obtaining my B.A. in Psychology—ONE class from my four-year degree!

Even with my family, I see the number of times I have "started" on a project or gift for someone (like photo projects, thank you notes, Christmas cards, etc.) only to not finish it. Why? I have been so afraid of succeeding over the years that I literally put these roadblocks up in my life and find reasons to justify that just chip away at me.

What I learned on this dive was how to break through—even if just a little at a time—and how AMAZING I felt when I accomplished this goal. I also learned an important lesson from my dive coach! I let go and surrendered, really trusted him, communicated without words underwater, listening and focusing on what works, and realized how his calmness gave me confidence to go again!

The biggest lesson I learned was that when I DIVE IN (literally) with all of me and focus on finishing, calling forth the good qualities that I know I have (calming, confidence, determination, focus, excitement), and FOCUS on the good, how much simpler things can be. This really made me think about what other opportunities I have missed out on by giving up and not believing in myself—or not getting through my limiting beliefs. I can say with an open heart that, if it wasn't for me setting this goal, I would not have had an opportunity to realize this—and what a blessing that is! 〞

- Mandi Ross

Setting and accomplishing goals is a key component to high self-esteem. Most people have goals and dreams, and yet few are determined and focused about goal setting and goal accomplishment. Few set goals that are worthy of them—goals that elevate their thinking, their results, their self-esteem.

When you set goals, consider the questions, "What do I want? What do I want to create?" Not what you don't want. It's easy for most people to tell you what they don't want. It is not very powerful to set goals or to build a life around what you don't want. For example, setting a goal around not being overweight is not nearly as powerful as setting a goal around creating a healthy and strong body.

"There is a profound difference between problem solving and creating. Problem solving is taking an action to have something go away—the problem. Creating is taking action to have something come into being—the creation. Most of us have been raised in a tradition of problem solving, and have had little real exposure to the creative process. What motivates a creator? The desire for the creation to exist."

- ROBERT FRITZ -

YOUR WHY

Any goal has to have a "why" behind it—a compelling why—so that on the days that your limiting beliefs are in full force or you hear *no*, you can get back up, dust yourself off, and keep going. You will be able to keep moving because what you want is bigger than the *no* and your limiting beliefs.

For instance, a goal to create $50,000 in income in 90 days is great. It's even more powerful if your *why* is that the $50,000 will create your first investment in bringing in passive income, your first step in your future lifestyle of liberty. When you set a money goal, what are you going to do with the money? Buy a car or a house? Go on vacation? Get specific. When you accomplish your goal, what will that mean about you? Who is the man or woman that you will become in the process?

It's not necessarily about making $50,000, it's about what you are now going to do because you made $50,000. Make your goal mean something. Set a goal, that when achieved, your life will be significantly different.

Tracy set a goal to clean out her garage. How could a clean garage be a big goal? How would cleaning out her garage fundamentally change who she was? After getting grief from some of her peers about her "weak" goal, she revealed to all of us that her husband had passed away five years earlier, and she needed to clean out his things from their garage to move forward in her grief and in her life. *That* is a big *why* behind a goal.

S.M.A.R.T.

First, set your goal using the S.M.A.R.T. model:

S—Specific

Goals must be specific in nature so that you—and everyone else—know precisely what you are going to accomplish. "Make more money" is a nice goal, but it is not specific enough because even making $1 more means you will have made more money and achieved your goal. "Make $500 more this month" is specific; you will know precisely if you accomplish this goal or not.

Do not limit yourself though. "Earn $500 more in 30 days *by selling real estate*" is specific, but it limits your ability to earn that money through any and all means that the Universe is willing to provide you. Do you care if the money comes exclusively from real estate? Let the Universe decide how it's going to happen. Do not include *the who* and *the how* in the goal.

> "It's kind of strange, but first you have to know what you want, defined in terms of the end result. And then you have to physically move towards it, without defining the hows.
>
> At which point, the thing you want actually starts coming to you, on its own terms, from a direction completely unexpected.
>
> Not unlike a cat."
>
> - THE UNIVERSE -

M—Measurable

It is very important that you set a goal that is measurable. A measurable goal has a clearly defined end result. When you have a measurable goal, you are able to gauge your progress, and you know if and when you've achieved the goal. You want to write your goal in such a way that anyone in the world could read it and be able to measure whether you have achieved it. "To be happier" is not a measurable goal. We are not able to measure whether you are happier. "To be more patient" is not a measurable goal. You can, however, measure the actions that you take that will result in feeling happier and more patient. Such as, "Spend one hour each day reading something I love." Or, "Wake up one hour earlier, at 6:30 a.m. so I have time to enjoy my children in the morning." These goals are measurable.

A—Attainable

While you need to set a BIG goal, it also must be attainable and achievable. You want to shoot for success while also playing a big game. Yes, it is *possible* to meet the woman of your dreams and be in a committed, monogamous relationship in 90 days. However, if you haven't been on a date in three years, maybe you can start with a dating goal.

R—Risky

A goal without risk is more like a to-do action item. In order for a goal to be worthy of you, it must entail some risk. Otherwise, why do you want it? Why haven't you already accomplished it? You will know you have a risky goal because your emotions will speak to you. You will feel your heart race, you may feel sick to your stomach; you will have a physical reaction, and your limiting beliefs will be screaming!

T—Time Frame

Is it a 30-day goal? A 90-day goal? It is very important for you to include a specific end date for the goal to be accomplished. Lock yourself in. When you lock yourself in, something really great happens. *You create tension and stress. Tension and stress are a goal achiever's friend.* Nothing great was built without them.

In his book, *The Path of Least Resistance*, Robert Fritz writes, "One basic principle found throughout nature is this: tension seeks resolution. From the spider web to the human body, from the formation of galaxies to the shifts of continents, from the swing of pendulums to the movement of wind-up toys, tension-resolution systems are in play. When someone asks you a question, you resolve the tension by answering the question."

Fritz uses the example of a rubber band. "If you stretch a rubber band, the tendency of the rubber band is to pull back to resolve the tension in the structure." Tension seeking resolution can be applied to goal setting. The tension is created by the gap, the discrepancy between your current results and the end result of your goal.

This discrepancy causes stress, turmoil—a perturbed state. This leads to strategizing, planning, preparing, and creativity, which leads to action, wins and failures, learning and experiences, new options, and solutions, which lead to the completion of the goal. Tension seeks resolution. Embrace the tension or, at least, understand its value!

Think of a time frame that is BOTH attainable AND risky.

> "To achieve great things, two things are needed; a plan, and not quite enough time."
> - LEONARD BERNSTEIN -

EXAMPLE GOALS

In 90 days, I will weigh 120 pounds and have 25% body fat.

Over 90 days, my significant other and I will have 12 dates that are at least two hours long, with no outside distractions, including technology.

I will complete three official 5k races in the next 90 days.

I will create $50,000 of income from a new source in the next 12 months.

Set a S.M.A.R.T. goal. Specific, Measurable, Attainable, Risky, Time Frame?

_____

_____

_____

_____

_____

UNREASONABLE ACTIONS

Unreasonable results require unreasonable actions. Your current results are reasonable; your new goal is unreasonable—according to your thinking. Therefore, you have to be willing to take unreasonable actions. In the last 19 years, I have witnessed *thousands* of people set unreasonable goals and get really excited about the end result of achieving them. Then, I watch them do very reasonable things day after day, expecting unreasonable results.

If you want unreasonable results, you have to get committed to unreasonable actions. This seems like common sense, but because of our strong neural pathways and commitment to doing it our way, it is not common sense. If you really look at unreasonable actions, they include:

- Doing actions you have NEVER done before.
- Being scared and doing it anyway: scary phone calls, meetings, confrontations.
- Doing actions that don't fit your beliefs about you.
- Completing actions that will cause your limiting beliefs and negative self-talk to be present.
- Taking actions and exhibiting behavior that people will judge.
- Doing things that are not convenient, practical, appropriate, or normal.

All of these must be done over and over and over. If you do what you have always done, you will continue to get what you always get. Imagine if you had a habit of doing the above items and how that would serve your self-esteem. Look at your goal, and answer the following questions:

- What actions are you willing to do to get this goal that you have NEVER done before?

- What is it that you are scared to do, yet willing to do anyway?

- What are the actions that you are committed to doing that other people will judge?

- What actions are you willing to take that are inconvenient, impractical, and abnormal?

I have a friend, Addy, who was really tired of being single and was doing all of the "reasonable" things to get a good date, find a good boyfriend, maybe even a husband. She tried dating websites, speed dating, even asking out men she found interesting. Yet, she still had this big, juicy goal of a fulfilling dating life.

So, she did something outrageous, something completely unreasonable: she gathered together all of the contacts she had in her database—every person she knew, be it family, friend, professional contact, colleague, even people that she really didn't know but had met in passing—and she sent them an email.

The email was titled, "The Great Date Game," and in it, she challenged every single one of them to compete against each other over the next 12 months to set her up on the best date ever. The winner would get a plane ticket to Vegas. Was it reasonable? No. Was it outrageous? Yes. Did she have the best dating year of her life? Yes!

When you pursue a big, juicy goal, be willing to do unreasonable things—whether these things directly affect your goal or not.

Imagine Monica, who has a goal to record her first album and double her income. Do you see that Monica going skydiving will support both of these goals, even though skydiving has nothing to do with either of these goals?

When you are willing to do something scary, anything scary, you change your vibration, your energy. Monica is very scared of her big money goal and of skydiving, and neither fit her limiting beliefs. When she realizes that skydiving is not too large to accomplish, then she has more evidence that maybe accomplishing the big money goal is possible, also. Every cell in her body is now alive and awake. That can be effective when going after goals and increasing self-esteem.

Adopt an unreasonable mindset everywhere. Everything speaks; it all contributes. Do things that will give you a physical reaction— where your limiting beliefs are screaming at you, and you do it anyway, like skydiving, singing karaoke, asking out a gorgeous woman, or kidnapping your significant other. Be outrageous. Do things that you are scared to do. Why? Because if those things are not bigger than you, what else is not bigger than you?

> "The best way to gain self-confidence is to do what you are afraid to do."
> - WILLIAM JENNINGS BRYAN -

FAILURE

Recognize that failure is part of success. When you achieve your goal and sell x, y, and z, how many *no*'s will you have heard along the way? The only way to get better is to practice, and there is no way around it. Anybody who is really good at something spent dozens, if not hundreds, of hours practicing that something and failed at that something over and over again. It may feel like failure, yet with every repetition, beliefs are changing, which are changing habits, which are changing neural pathways.

Be willing to fail forward. If you knew that getting over the hump was going to require 100 failures and that on attempt 101 you'd succeed, how quickly would you get through those failures to get to success? What if success was guaranteed, but you needed to fail and fail and fail and fail until you reached it? Would you get motivated—even excited about—those failures?

In baseball, a good batting average is .300, which means that out of 1,000 times at bat, the player hits the ball successfully only 300 times. This means that they fail the other 700 times; they fail 70% of the time. In 1923, Babe Ruth set the record for the most home runs in a season, while also striking out more than any other player in Major League Baseball. Ruth struck out 1,330 times over his entire career, but still hit 714 home runs.

> "I've missed more than 9,000 shots in my career. I've lost almost 300 games. Twenty-six times, I've been trusted to take the game winning shot and missed. I've failed over and over and over again in my life. And that is why I succeed."
>
> - MICHAEL JORDAN -

CHICKEN EXITS

Have you ever been in line to ride a really scary rollercoaster? As you wait in the very long line, you watch people get on and you watch people get off; many look very different than when they got on. Your stomach starts churning; your anxiety rises. Just as you get to the front of the line you see the *chicken exit*, your escape back to safe and comfortable. For a split second, you consider ducking through the gate, because no one will know. Then you hear your

10-year-old son ask, "Are you excited, Mom?" and the chicken exit is no longer an option.

Chicken exits are any reasons, excuses, loopholes, and limiting beliefs that allow you to quit the goal when you get scared, and sometimes before you even get started. Develop a foolproof plan so that if you go on autopilot or want to quit, the goal is accomplished anyway. Close off the chicken exits—such as not telling anyone about your goal so it's easier to quit—and set yourself up for success.

Your limiting beliefs (your ways of thinking) are slippery little fish that are masters at keeping you exactly where you are and preventing you from achieving your goals. Your limiting beliefs are VERY committed to staying alive and running the show, just like you. They become very solution-oriented, coming up with new and different ways to keep themselves alive and kicking—reasons and excuses and new distractions.

Excuses are limiting beliefs in disguise. They might disguise themselves in old dramas, new dramas, or urgent needs in other areas of your life. They may convince you that you're not interested in the original goal, that it doesn't matter anyway; things are fine. Or they could show up as an overwhelming disbelief in yourself, communicating things like, "Who do you think you are? You can't do that!" Or, perhaps, they'll look like some shiny new object that seems more worth the chase—the bait and switch. These are some of the chicken exits that you will be closing. Competing against your well-established brain and its current neural pathways is no small endeavor.

Write a list of your most common chicken exits and excuses.

Chicken Exit #1: _____

Chicken Exit #2: _____

Chicken Exit #3: _____

Chicken Exit #4: _____

Chicken Exit #5: _____

LOUD AND PROUD

Tell everyone you know about your goal. Everyone! Send an
e-mail to your database. Post it on Facebook. Put your butt on
the line. You will be extremely motivated to accomplish your goal
when you know people are watching whether you succeed or not.
Ask people to inquire about the progress of your goal. This can be
annoying, yet effective. When I know people are going to ask me
about my goal, like writing this book, I am much more likely to keep
taking steps so I have something to report.

Be accountable to someone on a weekly basis—a coworker, a boss,
or your significant other. Be loud and proud. Start conversations
about your goal. Tell everyone you know and everyone you meet.
They might have ideas and solutions. They might know somebody.
Many times, our solutions come from unlikely sources.

Pretend that any and every human being could be one degree of
separation from the person you need to achieve your goal. When you
tell your goal to everyone you know, you are locking it in even more.
You are creating even more of that effective tension and stress!

TRIGGERS

Use triggers to constantly remind you of your goal, the more the
better. When you go on autopilot, avoid, or become busy, you can be
triggered back to your goal. Whatever you focus on grows. Triggers
can be anything: a trophy, a pen, a piece of jewelry, a sign on the
wall. I love using signs, from big signs to sticky notes everywhere.

My signs are on the walls, the fridge, the computer, rearview mirror, bathroom mirror, the ceiling above my bed.

Post signs that make you laugh, stop you in your tracks, inspire you to take action, remind you of your goal, or cause you to pause and think and question: "Don't you dare open this cabinet," or "What are you avoiding?" or "10 more pounds to go!" or "What are you doing right now?" or "50 calls a day, what # are you on?" or "You can have great relationships or you can be right!" or "Suffering is optional." or "What are you eating?" or "What is one quick way I can like myself right now?" You might hang pictures of the end result of your goal: your future body, your house with a sold sign out front, or your new relationship.

My other favorite trigger is jewelry. When I set a new goal, I like to buy a new piece of jewelry that represents my goal. I like to buy rings or watches because they are easy to wear every day and I look at them often. Imagine if I touch that ring or look at it 20 times a day. What if every time I touch that piece of jewelry, I ask myself, "What is one small thing I could do to achieve my goal right now?" Or maybe, when I touch that jewelry, I remind myself I am worthy of my goal.

BREAK IT DOWN

Get serious and set yourself up to win. Be willing to look at your goal from every angle. Complete the following lists and answer the questions to help you prepare for your upcoming opportunities.

Make a list of 50 new ways of achieving your goal. Remember to be creative and *unreasonable* in this list. Write down everything that comes to mind. Clear your brain of all ideas, so you can create a vacuum for more.

1. _____

2. _____
3. _____
4. _____
5. _____
6. _____
7. _____
8. _____
9. _____
10. _____
11. _____
12. _____
13. _____
14. _____
15. _____
16. _____
17. _____
18. _____
19. _____
20. _____
21. _____
22. _____
23. _____
24. _____
25. _____
26. _____

27. _____
28. _____
29. _____
30. _____
31. _____
32._____
33. _____
34. _____
35. _____
36. _____
37. _____
38. _____
39. _____
40. _____
41. _____
42. _____
43. _____
44. _____
45. _____
46. _____
47. _____
48. _____
49. _____
50. _____

Make a list of the 10 things that you are willing to do now, things that
you have been unwilling to do in the past. What are you willing to
do differently to achieve the goal? Maybe you're willing to do a strip
tease for your wife to jazz up your marriage. Maybe you'll start your
own Great Date Game like Addy and operate outside of your comfort
zone. Are you willing to track your expenses? Are you willing to
experience a different form of exercise? Are you willing to take a class
on online marketing? Are you willing to wake up at 5:00 a.m.? Are
you willing to call 10 people and ask for new ideas?

1. _____
2. _____
3. _____
4. _____
5. _____
6. _____
7. _____
8. _____
9. _____
10. _____

Make a list of the 10 things that you are willing to stop doing,
to give up, to achieve the goal. Maybe you are willing to give up
alcohol because when you drink at night you neglect to get up in the
morning to work out. Maybe you are willing to give up video games,
fast food, your favorite TV show, taking naps, gossiping, Facebook,
or your negative friends.

1. _____
2. _____

3. _____

4. _____

5. _____

6. _____

7. _____

8. _____

9. _____

10. _____

Make a list of 10 prices you are willing to pay to achieve the goal. There will always be prices; know what they are in advance. You don't create a toned, muscular body without paying prices. You don't create great financial results without paying prices. Maybe you are willing to stay up later with your significant other and miss some much-coveted sleep so you can work on your relationship. Maybe you are willing to miss some of your children's games in order to finish your degree. Maybe you are willing to spend more time working out and less time getting ready in the morning. Maybe you are willing to sacrifice making money in order to travel. Other possible prices you may be willing to pay in order to achieve your goal: less time going out with friends, having diet restrictions, having to say no if you are on a budget, less time at work, having to wake up early, being uncomfortable, or being sore from working out. Be willing to go through the struggle to get the goal. Be willing to pay the prices. Incorporate and plan for the prices. Celebrate and embrace the prices.

1. _____

2. _____

3. _____

4. _____

5. _____

6. _____

7. _____

8. _____

9. _____

10. _____

Be aware of your potential obstacles. Make a list of 10 possible obstacles to achieving your goal and how you will handle each one when they come up. Maybe what you thought was a done deal is not. Have a plan B, C, D through P. It is usually plan P that works; most people never get there. Maybe your ex-wife is not as flexible with switching weekends as you assumed she would be. Will you be victim to her, or do you have a backup plan? Maybe you don't get the funding from Source A, B, or C. Has somebody been working on plan D? Forecasting both success and failure will always make it even more possible to be successful because you are prepared for pitfalls and setbacks.

1. _____

2. _____

3. _____

4. _____

5. _____

6. _____

7. _____

8. _____

9. _____

10. _____

How do you eat an elephant? If you've set a large goal over time, back into the goal by breaking it down into pieces such as weekly or monthly. Your goal is to create $50,000 in 90 days, and you are going to do that by selling widgets. How many total widgets do you need to sell? How many per month? Per week? Per day? How many phone calls per day to get those sales? How many presentations each week? How many lunches? How many people do you need to be in front of? Think of your goal in terms of the small stuff that, layer upon layer, will lead to the big stuff.

1. _____

2. _____

3. _____

4. _____

5. _____

6. _____

7. _____

8. _____

9. _____

10. _____

BE A BEGINNER

Be a student, be a learner, be willing to be a beginner. When you are willing to be a beginner, you experience growth. Where the comfort ends, the growth begins. There is nothing comfortable about being a beginner; it's new, clumsy, and unfamiliar. Imagine your first five golf lessons as a beginner. It's not pretty.

> "In times of change, the learners inherit the earth while the learned will find themselves beautifully equipped for a world that no longer exists."
> — ERIC HOFFER —

The learners take classes, lessons, workshops, and attend seminars; they are committed to learning. They move with the times and are flexible. The learners are willing to not know, to invest in themselves, to not stay safe and comfortable, and to take risks. The learned are the *know-it-alls*. You can't teach them anything new. They don't take risks. They are stuck and positioned about what used to work. Where have you been unwilling to be a beginner? Your current job, investments, dating, a new sport? Where are you willing to be a beginner now?

My husband is a great example of being willing to be a beginner. I have watched him climb to the next level numerous times, every time starting over as the low man on the totem pole. Yet he embraces being the low man because of the education, the learning, the people, and the experiences that come with it. He hires people smarter than himself. He is committed to surrounding himself with people who know more, do more, and have more.

> "If you're the smartest person in your group, then you need a new group."
> — LES BROWN —

Are you willing to be a learner? For life?

CHANGE YOUR PERSPECTIVE

*"You can complain because roses have thorns,
or you can rejoice because thorns have roses."*

- TOM WILSON -

Would you agree that life is going to keep happening? That there will be difficulties, obstacles, roadblocks, people, situations, and problems for the rest of your life? That is certain. It's not about what happens; it's about how you handle and how you respond to what happens. Driving both of those is your view of what happens.

There is value in changing your perspective. No matter what occurs, you can choose how you view it. You can choose to view it as an opportunity or doom and gloom. Have you ever been fired and immediately went to doom and gloom? Then, three days later, a new door opened and your view switched. Or at first you were devastated by a relationship breakup, and then, at some point, you got down on your knees in gratitude of the Universe's wisdom?

I am suggesting that you can skip the doom and gloom step and go straight to *"What an opportunity."* How you view things is simply a habit. Always focusing on the negative or what is wrong is a habit. Expecting the worst is simply a habit, as is expecting the best. Thinking the glass is half full is a habit, as is thinking the glass is half empty.

Oftentimes, it is simply our view that is in the way of achieving the goal. We often think that there is only one way to do something, our way, and when we do that over and over without success, we get frustrated, we get stuck, and sometimes we give up. When we are able to consider a different perspective, a different opinion or, even better, many different perspectives, a whole new world of solutions and resources is available. Then we are willing to change our approach. Do you want to be right about your way not working, or do you want to be successful?

Change your perspective, change the result.

Change your approach, change the result.

One day my sister had the opportunity to be enlightened by a different approach shown to her by her eight-year-old son, Enzo. Teachers come in countless forms. This is certainly not the first time profound learning has come from a child.

> **"** My daughter Kat struggles with spelling a lot. So one day with an hour to kill waiting for my son, Enzo, I decided we would work on the effects of the silent 'e.' We had time. We covered the vowels. We had a 'learning jingle' to help. I tried every way I knew how to get her to learn it. After 30 minutes, frustration set in, and I was yelling at her. How could she know it one time and then 10 seconds later get it wrong? Argghhhhh! Of course, she was upset and crying. Our hour was up, and Enzo gets in the car to a very tense situation. So, what do I do? I start on him. 'Enzo, I thought you were going to tutor your sister this summer?' He says, 'Okay, what were you were working on?' 'Silent e.'
>
> We get home, and he sets Kat up in a chair with a table and asks if she wants to play school. He then proceeds to ask if she is comfortable, and would she like him to get her some milk before they start? Wow. 'Yes!' says a happy Kat. Enzo works with her for 10 minutes and then says to me, 'What does she need to do to prove that she knows it?' Now I'm mad because clearly he is doing MUCH better than me, so I say, 'She has to spell 30 words and she has to get an A, so 90%.' He says, 'Okay.' He doesn't give me back talk, no 'That is ridiculous!' Just, 'Okay.' He administers the test, and even asks me (the principal, as I have been dubbed by now) to come up with the last 10 words for the test. The result was 27 out of 30 correct. Unbelievable! **"**

- Erin Cermak

If the approach you are using is not working, it is helpful to change your perspective and, hence, change your approach. Your perspective and approach are simply one way out of hundreds. Most people are attempting to force their "round" approach into a "square" hole. Most people are walking definitions of insanity—doing the same thing over and over expecting a different result. If you want a different result, do something different.

EXCHANGE OF VALUE

One brilliant way to achieve your goals is to help someone else with their goals. The key to living your dreams is to help someone else live their dreams. If you are willing to give the people in your life what they want, you will get what you want. It really is that simple.

However, most people are not willing to give until they get. The key is to go to the middle over and over, to give before you get. Most people stand on the sidelines waiting for the other person to change—they want to see evidence first. "When he does X, Y, and Z, then I might think about..." *No*. It doesn't work that way; you change *first*. Guide them to the middle. Be flexible. Compromise. Give. Or stay where you are and be right.

I am not talking about being a doormat, victim, or martyr. I am talking about giving where it will take nothing away from you to give. Where it will cost you nothing other than giving up your way. Think about places that you could be giving that you are not because you are holding a grudge, are holding back, thinking it should be different, thinking they should be different, or thinking they need to jump through a hoop first.

I am talking about giving because you can, because *givers give* and *givers gain*. Call your mother! I am talking about exchange of value. I am talking about doing the things that you might not necessarily like, things that might be inconvenient. Why? Because that is what they want. And why would you do that? So you get what you want.

In the process of exchanging value, there is a way of creating a win-win with our relationships that allows the space to continue increasing our self-esteem. It's amazing how you can add a little pep to your step when you are willing to be inconvenienced for the people you love. Why? Because you didn't have to and you did it anyway.

Who said you had to be happy and comfortable all the time? I was facilitating a seminar and asked the participants to think of something they could do that night to give to someone else. One man said he was going to call his mother, whose main joy is phone calls from her children. One person said she was going to buy the fancy colored pencils her son had been begging for; she didn't have a good reason for making him wait.

One woman said she was going to take her wife out for Indian food. She continued to explain that her wife's favorite food was Indian food, and that they had not been out for Indian food for nine years because she didn't like it. Seriously! Who said you had to be happy all the time?

There are plenty of things that I do with my husband that I don't necessarily enjoy. I go to sporting events with him. I ride in the golf cart while he plays golf. He loves his Harley, and so I agree to ride with him. I go to restaurants that do not interest me because that is where he wants to go.

I have spent countless hours wandering Costco because he loves practicing consumerism there. My husband is a consumer and is always willing to support the economy. I need to find value to part with my dollars. Through appreciating and learning from each other, somehow we meet in the middle. I have learned to spend more. He has learned to save more. It's part of the give and take of being in a relationship.

My husband brings me home a Starbucks coffee every morning.

Not some mornings, *every* morning he is in town. Before we had our daughter, my coffee would be in the kitchen before I woke up. (My husband is one of those people increasing his self-esteem at the gym at 4:30 a.m.; I am not.)

One day, he was at Starbucks before playing a round of golf with some friends. He told his friends that he would meet them at the golf course because he had to bring a coffee home for his wife. His buddy snorted derisively. "I almost got roped into that this morning, but I was smart." As he backed out the door, my husband replied, "One day you are going to learn: a happy wife is a happy life."

Sometimes people will go to the middle for a short time, give for a short time, and then call it quits. *See, it's not working.*

Change does not happen overnight. If you walk 12 miles into the jungle, you have to walk 12 miles out. It may have taken you 12 years to create the walls that exist. They will not be knocked down in three months. If you keep meeting in the middle, giving them what they want, over and over, eventually they will wake up, notice what is happening, and start participating.

At the beginning people are often leery. Will it work? Can they be different? Of course they can. They have habits, too. They are accustomed to things being a certain way. They can learn something different and create new habits, too. Sometimes we have to give the people in our lives a little more credit, and sometimes we have to let relationships go. I am not suggesting for you to stay in an abusive relationship. This is not the answer to all relationships, just the majority.

I received this e-mail from a woman who was participating in a 90-day program for achieving goals, which speaks eloquently about this concept:

66 All of my goals have provided amazing results in my life. I feel better about myself. I am more calm and grounded due to yoga. I have more money. However, the one that has been the greatest is the random acts of kindness for my husband. I am often going out of my way doing little things: leaving him notes, biting my tongue when I want to be right (or know that I am right, hee hee), or planning romantic things. This has been amazing for our relationship. I was treated to a Sunday where I was pampered all day long; he has picked up the slack with washing clothes and figuring out meals while I've been busy with my goals. He has now left many cards in my car or under my pillow, and today I got a dozen roses just because he wanted to prove I'm not the only one who could do random acts of kindness to improve our relationship. I am crying as I write this, knowing that my relationship is at a completely different level because of me. It's one of those priceless things that you get from doing this kind of work on yourself that you'd never give back. 99

- Renae Rochon

One of Renae's teammates read her e-mail and responded with this:

66 Renae's email reminded me how things have come full circle at my house, too, with giving to my sons. My son Cody works and pays for his own car insurance and gas. I filled up his tank and have given him gas money a few times in the last month, which made him so surprised and so appreciative. I find he is so willing to do things for me like fixing the lawnmower, doing yard work last weekend, and running errands, too. And the other day my son Brogan knew my shoulder was really hurting me, so he gave me a massage after work. Later on, he heard me saying how much it was hurting and he stopped in the middle of playing Xbox and gave me another quick 10-minute massage again. For him to pull away from a video game to do this for me? That was priceless. 99

- Kelli Allan

Be willing to give people what they want, not what you think they should have. This goes for business, too. Do you want to give your clients what you think they should want, or what they actually want? It seems silly, yet a majority of people are more committed to doing it, selling it, packaging it, distributing it, communicating it, and leading it their way than being committed to the end result called bringing value, making sales, and making money.

THE $1 MILLION CONCEPT

The $1 million concept is powerful. It is a game changer and can be a catalyst to achieving goals. Let's say you set up four 90-day goals that fit the S.M.A.R.T. method. These are goals that require copious small actions to change your habits, to get new results, to improve your self-esteem. On Day 85, we check in on your progress with your goals. You would probably have plenty of reasons why you are where you are. Some of them might be reasons why you are not going to reach your goals.

What if you had been told on Day 1 that you would receive a million dollars on Day 90, upon the completion of your goals? Ask yourself:

Would the last 85 days look different?

What would have been different?

What would you have been willing to do that you weren't willing to do?

Who would you have opened your mouth to that you didn't?

Which commitments/deadlines would you not have broken?

How many more appointments, phone calls, networking opportunities would you have made?

Would you have cared what anyone else thought?

Where would you not have been victim to circumstance? Blaming traffic, kids, or other people?

Would failure have been an option?

The answer to all of these questions is why you don't have a million dollars. (And if you do have a million dollars, then this is why you don't have $10 million.) The gap between what you did versus what you would do is where all of your money is, where all of your answers are. *The reason you don't have a million dollars is because you are not willing to do the things you would do if the million dollars were on the line.*

It's the way you live your life. It's your mindset. What you do here is what you do everywhere. Failure is an option or failure is not an option; both are mindsets. Whichever mindset you have—you have it everywhere. If a million dollars is not important to you, consider this: this is also why you don't have million-dollar relationships, a million-dollar self-esteem, a million-dollar vision, or even million-dollar dreams.

This is what they mean by fake it until you make it. If you were willing to adopt the millionaire mindset and do the things you would do if the million dollars were on the line, watch how fast you would become a millionaire.

What if you treated yourself like a mortgage company, your boss, the IRS, or the grocery store treats you? They don't care what happened; your reasons and excuses do not interest them and have no bearing on the outcome.

I once heard someone say, "Well, as long as I learned something, that's all that matters." If you went to your boss and said, "Boss, I did not bring in the result that I committed to, however, I learned something." Will your boss agree that learning is all that matters? No. Your boss wants results.

"Dear Mortgage Company, I do not have the money to pay you

this month. Let me tell you what happened..." Will they care about your reasons and excuses? You are in line at the cashier at the grocery store: "I did the best I could this month, and I don't have any money for groceries. Can I just have these?" Most people treat themselves like they would their elderly neighbor or their sick friend. "It's okay, you'll do better next time. You have really good reasons for your failures. A for effort!"

COMMITMENT LADDER

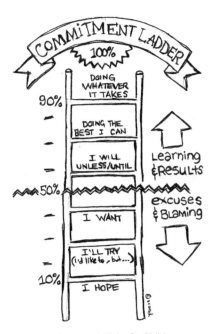

Original concept by John R. Childress

The rungs on the Commitment Ladder represent an increasingly greater level of commitment. The bottom rung is "I hope," as in *I hope I will be successful, yet probably not.* The next rung up is "I would like to but," as in *I would like to be successful, but I don't have a college degree.* Then there is "I will try," as in *I will try to be successful, but look at my track record.* Above that is "I want," as in *I want to be successful, I really do!* The next rung up is "I will until or unless," as in *I will be successful until the interest rates rise.* Or, *I will be successful unless the housing market crashes again.*

Then there is "I will do the best I can," as in *I will do the best I can to be successful, but it still might not be enough.* And the top rung is "I will do whatever it takes," as in *I will do whatever it takes to be successful. Nothing will stop me. Nothing.* These are mindsets; these are how people live their lives.

You live on one of these rungs of the ladder the majority of the time. Clearly the results produced from a mindset of "I hope" are different than the results produced from "I want," which are even more different than the results produced from the mindset of "I will do whatever it takes."

Which rung of the commitment ladder to do you live on the majority of the time? _____

Remember the self-esteem meter? Your level of self-esteem is driving where you live on the commitment ladder. When you increase your self-esteem, you will move higher on the ladder. If you live from a 45 on the self-esteem meter, then you predominantly live from "I want" on the Commitment Ladder. Notice the corresponding self-esteem percentages on the Commitment Ladder. When you increase your self-esteem to 60, "I want" will no longer be good enough; it will no longer fit.

You will realize that you are more powerful than "I want" as you move to "I will until or unless." Now you are causal and committed, depending on the conditions. When you increase your self-esteem to 80 you will no longer tolerate "I will until or unless"; it will no longer fit what you know about your capabilities. And you move to the mindset of "I will do the best I can."

People with a self-esteem of 90 to 100 operate from "I will do whatever it takes" in all areas of their life, not just some. They are not victim to outside circumstances, conditions, people, or technology. They know that they are the predominant creative force in their life.

Living anywhere beneath the rung of "I will do whatever it takes" is living from some form of victim consciousness. Even "I am doing the best that I can, but...the manufacturer, the Internet, someone, or something stopped me," is still victim to circumstance. There is still a big difference between "I will do the best I can" and "I will do whatever it takes."

I often ask people this question: if a $100,000 bonus were on the line, do you want to work with someone who does whatever it takes (assuming legal, moral, ethical) or someone who does the best they can? Inevitably, the answer is *I want to work with someone who does whatever it takes.*

People who operate from the rung of the ladder called "doing whatever it takes" also want to work with people who *do whatever it takes!* People who do whatever it takes do not want to work with people who do *the best they can.* When you are doing the best that you can, there is room for reasons, excuses, and justifications—which are all self-esteem chippers.

When you are doing whatever it takes, there is no wiggle room. We are talking about people who are able to produce a result when they have to, versus when they feel like it—people with high self-esteem. It's easy to produce a result when you feel like it. It's way more valuable to be able to produce a result when you have to.

Do you want to be a successful goal achiever? I recommend you check in daily as to where you stand on the Commitment Ladder in regards to your goal.

Matt has a goal to wake up at 6:00 a.m. and run a minimum of three miles every morning for 60 days. Matt's results are going to

HOW TO BE YOUR BIGGEST FAN!

depend on which rung of the Commitment Ladder he chooses the majority of the time. On day three he hears himself thinking, "I hope I wake up on time to run tomorrow."

Matt can stay on the lowest rung and "hope away" or he can get up and set five alarms to ensure success. On day 14 he might hear himself say, "I would really like to run tomorrow morning, but my daughter has to be at a special practice at 7:00 a.m. and it's a 45-minute drive." Matt can stay on the second-to-lowest rung and "like away" or he can call his sister and ask for help.

On day 21, Matt catches himself saying, "I am going to try to run in the morning, but I am working really late tonight." Matt can "try away" or he can tell his girlfriend that no matter what he says or does at 6:00 a.m., she has to get him up.

On day 35, Matt wakes up thinking, "I really want to achieve this goal, but I am so tired and I think I have shin splints." He can "want away" or he can look up and see the Commitment Ladder posted on his ceiling, see which rung he is choosing, and get up and go.

On day 44, Matt hears himself thinking, "I will run tomorrow unless it is raining. And if it is not raining then I will run until it starts raining." Matt can "unless or until away" or he can plan how he is going to run in the rain with the least amount of discomfort.

On day 50, Matt's five-year-old daughter asks how he is doing on his goal. He hears himself say, "Well, sweetie, I am doing the best I can; but I know I have to miss one day next week." Matt can "best away" or he can figure out how to be in integrity with the next 10 days. The only way Matt can say that he is willing to do whatever it takes is if he goes running every single day.

ACTION

The best thing you can do to get to your goal is to get into action—massive action. Stop thinking about it. Stop getting ready to get ready. Stop planning. Your whole life led you up to this moment. You are ready. You are prepared.

When a mama duck wants to get all of her ducklings moving, what does she do? Does she get all of her ducks in a row first? No. Does she ask the ducklings what their opinions are? No. Mama duck starts moving and all of her ducklings fall in line behind her.

When you start moving—and keep moving—everything you need will line up behind you. Will you be scared? Of course! Nobody has ever done anything great or new or different without fear being present.

This is beautifully explained by Steve Chandler in his book *Reinventing Yourself*:

> 66 The power and courage to do something often shows up halfway into the doing of the thing, not up front. 'Do the thing,' said Ralph Waldo Emerson, 'and you shall have the power.' The action itself is the source of the courage. Doing it is what erases the fear of doing it.
>
> "How can I motivate myself to sell more?" a salesperson asks. "By making a sale," I reply. "Well that's just it: I'm too low on motivation to do that. How do I get my motivation level up to where I want it so that I can make a sale?" "Get right into making the sale, and your motivation will go right up where you want it."
>
> That sounds like double-talk to the salesperson. So, I often use an exercise metaphor.
>
> "How do I motivate myself to run in the morning?"
>
> "By running in the morning."
>
> "But I don't feel like running."

"That's because you're not running yet. If you were running, pretty soon you would feel like running."

Fear is overcome by doing what we fear to do. Action defeats fear, just as scissors cut paper. And paper covers rock, and rock crushes scissors. It's the circle of life. But you've got to start it yourself. It won't happen on its own. **”**

CHAPTER EIGHT
TIPS TO LIGHTEN THE LOAD

"Those who achieve great things, defeat long odds, and become legends didn't have anything you don't have. They just kept showing up, expecting a miracle, long after everyone else got practical. Here comes one now...!"

- THE UNIVERSE -

About a year ago, I needed a favor from a friend. I told her if she helped me, I would make it worth her while. My friend had a dating goal, so I knew I would be safe if I set her up on a date. However, I wanted to show her an example of unreasonable and give her a night that she would never forget.

So, one day, when I had a block of time and some cocreative people around, I called her and asked if she was available that night. She said she was. I said, "Good, because you are going to be very busy tonight. You will be having four dates with four different men tonight."

Now, at the time I told her that, I had no idea who the men were going to be or any of the details. I just knew I would make it happen. She had a date with Mark at Starbucks at 5:30 p.m., Charles at Blanco's at 6:45 p.m., Ian at The Gelato Spot at 8:30 p.m., and Phil at The Second Story at 9:45 p.m. Here is Angela's recounting:

    " When I was first asked if I would be open to going on blind dates—my first thought was "Of course!" Then, as the opportunity unfolded, it became a series of blind dates. One right after the other. Oh, and I knew nothing about the guys, except their first name and where I was meeting them. What happened then? Anxiety! One blind date, okay; four blind dates? No. Hell no! Okay, maybe. Actually, it might be fun. Aw, what the hell...let's have an adventure! I went through a whole rainbow of emotions starting with resistance and nervousness, then ultimately to just surrender and have a good time. What occurred to me through the experience is that I assigned too much significance to the idea of a 'date.' It's not a proposal, not a job interview, not something that had to lead beyond that night. Just an opportunity to share a moment with another human being.

I also realized that in many areas of my life I tend to put so much focus on what will happen in the future that I often miss out on just being present in the moment. I had a great time that night with each of my dates, and what that taught me is that I don't have to overthink and analyze or know every detail—I don't have to be in control. In fact, since then—some of the most memorable and enjoyable times I have had are the times I let go of control and just went with the flow. Bonus: I NEVER have first date anxiety anymore!

Most importantly, that night has served as some very powerful evidence of what I am capable of, even if I am nervous, afraid, or insecure. Since then, I have taken a lot of risks that I would never have attempted out of fear of being ridiculed or making the 'wrong' decision. My definition of unreasonable action has shifted drastically, along with my commitment to creating an extraordinary life. I have learned that a truly great life doesn't just happen to those who stay safely tucked within their comfort zones. I must be willing to get through any fears or doubt and surrender to the unreasonable, wherever I can find it. It's a fun story I have shared with just about all of my friends and family, simply because it was unreasonable. "Who does that?" And it has inspired a few of them to say "Yes" to the unfamiliar, too! Of course, there are quite a few who reply, "Oh, I would NEVER do that!" and in that moment, I am just so grateful that isn't me anymore! 99

- Angela Cook

"Well-behaved women rarely make history."

- UNKNOWN -

SAY NO TO NORMAL, COMMON, AND REASONABLE

> "If you get up in the morning expecting to have a bad day, you'd rarely
> disappoint yourself. Stop complaining! Differentiate yourself from your
> competition. Don't be a duck. Be an eagle. Ducks quack and complain.
> Eagles soar above the crowd."
>
> - WAYNE DYER -

Most people live from the normal, common, reasonable,
appropriate, logical, and practical. It is *normal* to make $50,000 a
year, have credit card debt, and not plan for retirement. It is *common*
to justify, blame, and make excuses. It is *normal* to be overweight, to
self-medicate, and to not like yourself. It is *reasonable* to go after small
goals, play it safe, and not risk. It is *appropriate* to let men lead, wait
for a call back, and not rock the boat. It is *practical* to work for the
same company for 20 years and to plan, research, and get ready to
get ready to change careers the whole time.

So, how do you get out of that? *Do the abnormal, uncommon,
unreasonable, and outrageous.* Separate yourself. Get noticed. It is
abnormal to not participate in gossip, to take a stand for your values,
and be a leader. It is *uncommon* to keep your agreements and be
impeccable with your word. It is *unreasonable* to go on four dates in
one night, spontaneously go to Europe, or to fly somewhere for
dinner with a friend just for the night. It is *inappropriate* to buy a piece
of jewelry without looking at the price tag. It is *abnormal* to acquire
wealth, impact the community, and leave a legacy. Every one of
these unreasonable actions will give huge boosts to your self-esteem.

*Get committed to unreasonable, abnormal, and uncommon. Separate yourself
from most people.*

My family recently vacationed in Bethany Beach, Delaware. My
sister, who owns an event production company, decided to test out

one of her new ideas on my family, which she commonly does. She created a life-size game of Sorry to be played on the beach.

Do you remember the game Sorry with red, blue, green, and yellow teams? The object is to "get out" and make it all the way around the board to the safety of home base without being "Sorried" or knocked out by another player landing on your piece. Each color has four pieces to get around the board.

So, in the life-size game, my family members (aged 7 to 76) were the game pieces; hula hoops and beach chairs were used to create the game board. There we were wearing our team's color, cocktails in hand, hopping around the board. If somebody knocked you off the board, they got to tackle you to the sand to claim their spot. We had so much fun that we played another day and invited other families to join us.

Many of the people I invited had noticed us the first day and were very interested to know what we were doing. Of course, they wanted to leave their normal happy hour to join the fun. There was nothing practical about playing a life-size game of Sorry on the beach, which is why people wanted to join us.

Commit to one action you will take to be outrageous today.

WHO CARES WHAT OTHER PEOPLE THINK?

Realize that with anything you do in the world, 50% of the people will back you and 50% will oppose you. So, why base your self-worth and determine your actions based on what others think? In fact, as soon as you take on a position of leadership, you have already separated yourself from the masses, thereby creating opposition.

As you start climbing your personal mountain of success (and higher self-esteem), you expose yourself to the pessimists of the world. You become an easy target, and people are always going to throw darts at you. Why? Because it's easy to take shots from the cheap seats. It's easier for people to judge you, rather than look at themselves and change.

Have you ever seen a person sitting in a chair making fun of the people on the dance floor? Have *you* ever been guilty of this? Or have you ever thrown darts at the leader simply because you weren't the leader? Often, when people make critical judgments and throw darts at you, it's actually a sign that YOU are making positive progress. It means you are doing something different, maybe something outrageous, unreasonable, or uncommon.

When this happens, just keep moving! The higher you climb, the worse their aim becomes. Eventually, those people can't reach you anymore. They will find new targets, and you'll find yourself joining other like-minded individuals at the summit of the mountain.

> "You have enemies? Good. That means you've stood up for something, sometime in your life."
>
> - WINSTON CHURCHILL -

You have the option to spend your life on the sidelines, judging others, playing it safe, and living in fear, or you can step out onto the playing field and into the unknown and risk being judged. Only one of those options builds an extraordinary life of high self-esteem. As you increase your self-esteem, you will find that what other people think matters less and less.

> "What other people think about you is none of your business. How dare you care about what the neighbors think, they are not even thinking...I have talked to them."
>
> - BOB PROCTOR -

Think about this: some of the people, the ones you care about what they think of you, won't even be in your life five years from now. You spend five years caring about what the neighbors think, and then they move or you move and you never see them again. You spend 10 years caring about what your coworkers think, and then they get a new job or you start your own business and you never see them again. You allow your best friend's opinions to decide who you will date for three years, and then she gets married and moves to Paris. When you are 90, you will not remember these people's names. You will, however, remember what caring about their opinion cost you.

Identify three areas in your life where you are currently sitting on the sidelines:

1. _____

2. _____

3. _____

NAMING LIMITING BELIEFS

There was a gentleman who I was coaching, and we were discussing his limiting beliefs. He said, "I understand about limiting beliefs in theory, but what do I do when I hear that loud booming voice in my head that says I am not good enough?"

Name them and talk to them!

This exercise might sound crazy and feel weird, but it works. Sometimes, in my brain, it seems like there is a whole crowd of people talking and stating their opinion. Imagine that there are different parts of our brain run by our strongest limiting beliefs and non-limiting beliefs, like different territories run by Democrats and Republicans. I give each of the politicians a name and personality.

Remember the neural pathways that we strengthen and turn into highways? These "voices," these beliefs, determine the roads—sometimes superhighways, sometimes dirt roads—going to these territories. These are the six biggest limiting and non-limiting beliefs that currently hold space in my head.

Leroy runs the "I am stupid" territory.

Roxy runs the "I am brilliant" territory.

Captain Caveman runs the "I am not enough; I beat myself up so I play small" territory.

Shera runs the "I am enough; I can do anything" territory.

Sally runs the "Scarcity, I have to be frugal" territory.

Maximillian runs the "There is abundance, money flows freely" territory.

All of these beliefs are attempting to be helpful all of the time. These beliefs served me at some point, which is why I created them. If you have a belief that you can't trust people, that belief was created to protect you. Maybe it has served its purpose and is no longer needed. If you have a belief about scarcity, about there not being enough so you better get yours, that belief may have been created to protect you to ensure your survival.

As a result, you may be resourceful and good at saving money. Maybe you are finally done believing in the myth that there isn't enough. If you have a belief that you/things have to be perfect in order to not make anyone angry, that belief was created to keep you safe. You are probably a great planner, pay great attention to detail, and you can smile through anything. Maybe you are finally willing to retire your fake smile.

All of these beliefs were created to serve, benefit, protect, keep you safe, and make sure you survive. This may sound dramatic and serious. At the time, these beliefs were created when the situation was dramatic and serious; at least to you. Your limiting beliefs were created for your survival. The good news is you survived. The bad news is they are here to make sure you only survive.

Here are some tips to create a different relationship with your beliefs:

- Embrace all of your beliefs. They are on your side, they are rooting for you—but they are rooting for you in very different ways. Turn your enemy into your friend. After all, these are all parts of you. Embrace all parts of you; they all have a role to play.

- Name each of the beliefs and give them personalities, wardrobe, and dialogue. Separate them from yourself. They are just a small part of you that you can minimize and have fun with. You should hear some of the conversations I have with these people.

For example, Shera (I can do anything), of course, is dressed in leather and is tall, skinny, and sexy. She is a badass. She kicks anybody's butt that gets in her way. She will say what needs to be said, and she will do what needs to be done to produce the result. She also attracts other superheroes. She is a clear, direct, persistent, courageous powerhouse.

Sally (frugal/scarcity) looks like a librarian wearing a pencil skirt, glasses, and a bun—still sexy I might add. She runs the numbers, collects receipts, updates the spreadsheets, uses coupons, and looks for sales constantly. We need her, and we like to keep her quiet and busy. However, she can get loud and violent if necessary. She is protective, logical, practical, and reasonable. She says things like, "We can't afford that. We don't need that. We don't have enough to share."

Captain Caveman (I am not enough) is short and squat, wearing his caveman garb, dragging his club. He goes from zero to 60 fast. And when that club starts swinging...bam! "You're not good enough! You stink." Bam! "I told you we shouldn't have done that!" Bam! "You were wrong again!" Bam! "We are never doing that again. Do you hear me? It's too painful; that goal is too big for us." He is gruff, sarcastic, stubborn; he likes to be right and can be quite negative and protective.

- These voices—your beliefs—are working to help you survive. Each of them thinks that their job is the most important. Each of them thinks that doing things their way will help you the most. They are all going to do their job to the best of their ability. That's all they know how to do. Imagine you are in the middle of a conversation and someone pushes your button, or you have a situation you don't know how to handle. The voices fight to get the job, win the bid, be in charge, and do things their way.

- None of these beliefs are going away. Decide which of your beliefs you want to be in charge. Be proactive about which beliefs you are going to feed daily. You get to control how big their territory is and how much of a vote they have.

When I started my personal growth journey 19 years ago, Leroy (I am stupid), Captain Caveman (I am not enough), and Sally (frugal/scarcity) had very large territories. They were in charge, making the decisions, and loving it. I have since learned how to minimize their territories. I like Sally and I bring her out on purpose sometimes to help me organize big projects. She has much less of a vote now in my daily life. I certainly do not allow her to join me when I am shopping for jewelry or nice clothes.

We simply do not agree on how worthy I am. I am actively *not* feeding those territories, turning the highway back into a dirt road. They still show up, sometimes out of the blue. Occasionally, I will look up and find myself in the sale section, or I will chastise my husband for a purchase, and I know that Sally has snuck in.

Today Shera (I can do *anything*), Maximillian (*abundance*), and Roxy (I am *brilliant*) have very large territories. I am actively feeding those territories, creating neural superhighways to the ones I want to run the show; I am in control.

I remapped my beliefs through the small stuff: the daily, weekly, and monthly actions that set up new habits and new evidence— evidence that I can use to tell Leroy to stuff it. Evidence that I can use to show Sally that I don't need her as much. Evidence to show Shera that she has a place to thrive.

Let me give you an example of an interaction with my beliefs. I am not particularly fond of shopping for clothes, although I like nice clothes and I like to look good. My conscious brain makes the announcement to my subconscious brain that we are going shopping. All of those people/beliefs live in my subconscious brain. Immediately, the chaos begins. Everybody is yelling, shouting, and attempting to be heard. Everybody thinks that, clearly, they are the one to handle the job. By the way, our limiting beliefs are very persuasive. They are *persistent*, *passionate*, *sneaky*, and *driven*—they like being in control. Here's what you might hear in my brain:

Sally (frugal/scarcity): I don't think this is a good idea. Last week your husband spent $500 at Tommy Bahama. We should wait until next quarter, when it's fiscally responsible.

Maximillian (abundance): Screw that, let's go buy a mack daddy suit that makes us strut. You know that black one we wear? Like that. We have plenty of money, loads of it. What are we saving it for anyway? Let's go spend some of it and live in the now.

Captain Caveman (I am not enough): I don't know. Remember, we spent $650 on that suit Maximillian had to have, and we don't even wear it, except for those 25 times. We hate trying on clothes—remember the mirrors. We should stay home and shop online, it's safer. I don't want us to feel worse than we do right now.

Leroy (I am stupid): I don't like this idea. We always feel terrible after shopping. We know nothing about fashion. All those regrets. We are really not good at shopping, actually we stink at it. We have plenty of clothes in the closet, some with the tags still on, which proves we don't know what we are doing.

Roxy (I am brilliant): This is a great idea! We should get a personal shopper at Nordstrom's, sit down, and relax with a latte. We are brilliant, we deserve new clothes, and I think we are going to look good in those mirrors!

Shera (I can do anything): Oh, shopping! I love a good challenge! Step aside, I will save the day! Why are we still standing here? Let's go!

This is the short version. After the first round of opinions there is arguing, yelling, restating opinions, evidence, name calling, and past failures revisited. Now my conscious mind gets to take all of that information and make a decision. Who is going to win today? Who has the most voting rights? Sometimes the decision is to not make a decision. You can see why sometimes we are paralyzed, *getting ready to get ready*, working on it, and talking about it. There are a lot of opinions to sort through. Some people go to the movies to distract them. Some people self-medicate to put them to sleep.

Here is a great example of naming beliefs and changing perspectives and how both can impact self-esteem.

> 66 I travel almost every week. One thing that always used to bug me was when a fellow passenger brought a bag on board that they weren't able to stow, due to the fact that the bag was heavier and bigger than they were. This happened last week when I was traveling. Rather than going to the RED area of my thoughts, I leapt out of my middle seat with my 'Captain Invincible' cape and took control of the situation. I asked the nice lady if I had her permission to assist her with her shiny, red, 150-pound bag. With her permission, at the speed of light I began to reorganize the overcrowded storage bins. People were looking at me like I had escaped from an institution for former baggage handlers. Within seconds, the mission was accomplished and people were popping champagne and toasting to my success. It was AWESOME. I am a changed man; I found my inner strength and allowed myself to have FUN.
>
> The same thing happened to me yesterday morning when I was getting ready for a customer meeting in San Diego. I realized I had left my cufflinks at home. So, rather than freak out and go into deep panic, I went to CVS and enrolled a sleepy clerk to help me get creative in solving my rather minor problem. I left CVS with my dress shirt sleeves held together with white safety pins. That would never have happened in my former meetings. I would have called everyone I knew in San Diego before showing up to a meeting with a shirt held together with safety pins. My safety pins became my reminder of my inner strength versus an embarrassment. With that in mind, 'Captain Invincible' went on to seize the day. I am allowing myself to play the game of life BIGGER than I ever have. And it is awesome! 99

- Anton Visser

Think about two of your limiting beliefs and two of your non-limiting beliefs. Give them creative names.

Names for two of my limiting beliefs: _____

_____

Names for two of my non-limiting beliefs: _____

_____

THE DIP

Whenever you begin something new, it may feel uncomfortable at first. If you've ever started a new exercise regimen, you know how this feels: in the beginning, you're excited, anticipating a new, fit you. On day one, you hit the gym and are ready to work out. But within 10 minutes on the treadmill, you're gasping for air and wishing the workout was over. But you press on, determined to complete the goal you set for yourself.

By the time you walk out of the gym, everything feels great. You are energized and proud of yourself. On day two, you wake up a bit stiff. Your body isn't used to this new routine, and the spring in your step from day one has disappeared. You still go to the gym, but you're more tired today and can't muster the energy you had yesterday.

This routine continues for the next few weeks and, at times, you feel like giving up. What seemed like a good idea at the start now feels daunting and difficult. Your limiting belief is screaming for you to get back on the couch. Your new working out warlord is fighting for a foothold. You have a habit called *not working out for five years*. That neural pathway is huge, it's your go-to highway. Now you are going to change it?

Yes, you are committed. You come back day after day, even though your body hurts, your limiting beliefs are screaming; even though it would be easier not to, even though nobody would know, even though it's just a daily, small thing. Eventually you reach day 30. Your body hurts less, your limiting beliefs are screaming less, a new neural pathway is now more of a road and less of a dirt path, your self-talk is different, and you have begun a new habit.

The first 30 days of doing anything new, when comfort ends and growth begins, is what I refer to as *The Dip*. I spoke about *The Dip* for many years referencing a J curve, and then one day somebody showed me "The Change Process" online from Virginia Satir. As you can see from the picture, she was able to artistically communicate a concept I'd been using as a coaching tool all this time. There is nothing more uncomfortable than starting something new and doing something you have never done before, especially the first 30 days. If you can get through the first 30 days—*The Dip*—I believe you have a good shot at success. What this means is that you usually have to go down before you go up, you move further away before you move closer, experience chaos before you can move to effortless. You may become less effective and productive to become more effective and productive.

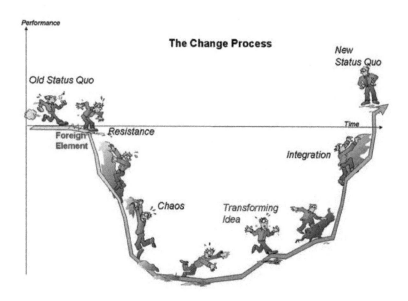

When you are in the first 30 days of anything, you are creating a new habit. You are retraining your brain. Think about the first 30 days of a new job, of dance lessons, of learning a new language, of hiring an assistant, or of working out. Why does it feel like sometimes you're going backwards? Why is it so difficult? Because you are doing something new.

There is no neural highway, only paths and dirt roads. You are traveling on dirt roads; they are bumpy, uncomfortable, and slow. Then you see the neural highways with big billboards and neon lights reminding you to come home, to safe and comfortable. Remember: your limiting beliefs have a very strong opinion about this new activity, and let's face it, we like to do things our way.

If you have been doing things a certain way for the last 10 years and now you are going to create a new habit, be prepared to spend some time, energy, and discipline during *The Dip*. Creating a new habit requires different actions and thinking. New habits don't just happen. Your commitment will be tested. You will be challenged. Your limiting beliefs will scream. *The Dip* is a good thing.

The Dip separates the interested from the committed.

There are plenty of people interested in making more money, interested in better physical health, and yet few are committed.

"There's a difference between interest and commitment.
When you're interested in doing something, you do it only
when it's convenient.
When you're committed to something, you accept no excuses; only results."
- KENNETH BLANCHARD -

I don't want you to be scared of *The Dip*; I want you to be prepared. I want you to find as many dips as possible. Being in the dip means that you are willing to be a beginner. If you are not uncomfortable somewhere, you are not growing. Keep being willing to be a beginner. It's one of our best qualities; it is highly underused.

The first 30 days is the beginning of a new habit and the hardest part. It's very important to continue the discipline through 90 days and beyond. I am amazed at what we can become accustomed to in 90 days. Anything!

When you are in *The Dip*, you are changing dirt roads into super-highways and changing old, useless superhighways back into dirt roads. You are choosing small actions daily, changing your habits, and creating new neural pathways that serve you and help you bring your best version to the world.

The know-it-alls refuse to go through *The Dip*. They are stuck just prior to *The Dip*. They're gathering evidence, justifications, and excuses. Every time you get to the other side of *The Dip*, you prove to yourself who is in charge, that "it" wasn't bigger than you, that quitting was not an option and, you guessed it, you increase your self-esteem.

20 PLATES SPINNING

I've met many people who set goals, then sabotaged their chances for success because they felt that everything had to be perfect—100% perfect— for them to start making progress. I knew a woman once who described herself as the type of person who always had to have a clean house. In fact, she shared that it needed to be so immaculate that you could eat off the bathroom floor. Literally!

About 30 days into working with her, she said to me, "I had a really big revelation that I would like to share. I have finally realized that no one wants to eat off my bathroom floor!" We all laughed, but her epiphany was profound, giving up her way was liberating. She's free to pursue other activities and goals, too. Of course, it's not as if she is now okay with a dirty house, but just relaxing her stance on this issue opened up time and space for her that she never had before.

I would rather have 20 plates spinning at 80% than one plate spinning at 100%. I would rather be able to have 20 things going well in my life than just one thing going perfectly, at 100%. I'd rather have a great marriage, be a fantastic parent, continue facilitating seminars, write my book, exercise, travel, and spend time with friends rather than focusing on just one of these areas to the exclusion of everything else.

Think of it as a beautiful hand-made quilt with many different (yet sometimes imperfect) squares—the squares being all of the unique, fun, adventurous people and activities in your life. Doesn't that sound better than limiting yourself?

When I mentioned plates spinning at 80% (imperfection), I do not mean only achieving 80% of the desired result. I'm not talking about half-hearted attempts or not working hard. I mean that you still get 100% of the result, yet you're not as concerned with the last 20% of the details, because those are usually the details that don't really matter in the end. Oftentimes, that 20% you stubbornly refuse to give up is just a matter of wanting things done in a certain way (*your* way) and not being flexible enough to realize there's a different way of doing things.

For example, organizing your office and insisting that your books have to be alphabetized by author's last name. You can have 100% of the result and value of an organized office, yet you did not spend two hours alphabetizing the books. Or preparing your child a healthy lunch and making sure every food item looks like an animal, as seen on the food channel. Instead, leave the food shaped as it is; your child can get 100% of the value of a healthy lunch, and you have 30 minutes to work out.

MY WAY VERSUS THE END RESULT

Have you ever been stuck wanting things to look a certain way? Have you ever thought that there was only one way—your way? Jessica is my favorite example of someone focused on doing things her way versus the end result. She is also an example of making sure the mechanism is perfect before action can begin. Jessica was part of a 90-day program for achieving goals. Her goals were to read the Bible, to write handwritten cards to family members, and to complete the "Insanity" workout program.

We were about three weeks into the program, and I asked her how reading the Bible was going; she had barely made any progress at all. When I checked in with her goal of sending out personal and handwritten cards to family members, she had made no progress. Finally, I checked in regarding her goal on completing the "Insanity" workouts, and you guessed it, there had been minimal progress.

I started with the cards. "Why have you not sent any cards?" I will never forget her response. She said, "I didn't have the right stationery." What? Next, I checked on the Bible goal. "Why is it you have made so little progress on the Bible?" She had decided that reading the Bible had to look a certain way. She had decided that when she read, no kids could be in the house, there had to be dim lighting with candles, and there had to be soft music playing in the background.

With four children, a busy life, and other commitments, can you see why it was almost impossible to ever find time to create these exacting circumstances? She was very serious. There is a "right" way to read the Bible. This might sound silly to some of you, yet somewhere you are probably doing the same thing. Her brain was not allowing her to see other options.

Clearly, there were infinite ways for Jessica to complete her three goals. However, she could only see one way—the way she had experienced in the past. People want to do things their way, and they like to be right about doing things their way. And, most of the time it is costing them what they say they want. There are people who would rather do things their way than have a great marriage.

There are people who are more committed to doing things their way than having a successful business. No matter what you want to accomplish, there are at least 100 ways to do it. Yours is just one way. It's not the right way or the best way, just one way. The only important consideration about your way is: will it get you the end result you want?

By the end of the program, Jessica was willing to give up her way, give up the way she thought it *should* look, and give up being right about it all. She decided to focus on the end result (her goals) versus the mechanism (how she accomplished them). She decided she would allow herself to "read" the Bible by listening to the audio version. She listened to the Bible *while* working out. The best part is, her kids could be home—even running around the house and screaming—while she did all of this.

She discovered that the right stationery was not nearly as important as what she wrote. As an added bonus, she's more fulfilled and has had more fun since she let go of how it had to look. She's been able to apply this mindset to other situations, too.

Done is better than perfect. Done is better than your way. If you stay focused on the end result and committed to the end result, you won't care how you got there (assuming you act legally, morally, and ethically).

Jessica is also a great example of learning about living a life of "and." At the beginning of going after her goals, she was thinking "either/or." I can either read the Bible or watch the kids, not both. I can either do my "Insanity" workout or read the Bible, not both.

Most people live their lives from this viewpoint. I can either go home for a family wedding or go on vacation, not both. I can either be a great mom or have a career, not both. When you are willing to give up your way and focus on the end result, you are open to thousands of possibilities and solutions that you could not see before. Then you'll see that living a life of "and" is possible. The truth was Jessica could complete her "Insanity" workouts *and* listen to the Bible *and* watch her kids, all at the same time. Once you learn how to operate from "and" you will never go back to "either/or." A big life requires the mindset of "and."

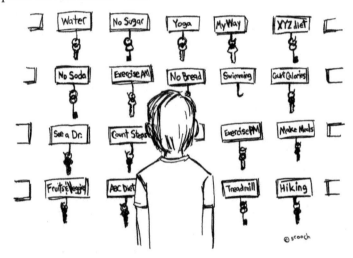

For years, my friend Kimberly wanted her mother to take a personal growth seminar. She expended a lot of time and energy in her strategies to enroll her mother. Finally, after three years, she was successful. When I ran into Kimberly two days before the seminar, she was hysterically upset. When I asked her what was wrong, she said, "My mother."

It turns out that Kimberly had created in her head a certain way that things should look when her mother took the seminar. Her mother *should* be staying at Kimberly's house, not at a cousin's house that is more convenient. Her mother *should* be flying out on Monday morning, not Sunday night. Her mother *should* be having meals with Kimberly, not making plans with friends. On and on she went.

It took me 30 minutes to get her to see that the only end result that mattered was her mother completing the seminar. Where she slept didn't matter, where she ate didn't matter, when she left didn't matter. When you get committed to the end result, you have to give up your agenda of how it should look. You can either be right about the way it *should* look, or right about the end result. Which will you choose?

Giving up your way = Giving up control = Surrender = Committed to the end result = Open to any solution = Bliss

In some areas of your life, just like in Jessica's and Kimberly's, your way is not the best way, not even close. People have been attempting to tell you this for years. The problem is they sugarcoat it. They say things like:

> Hey, I read this great book on Parenting, Focus, Procrastination. You should read it.
>
> Hey, what about John's idea? Maybe we should try that.
>
> You may want to try this diet or dating website.
>
> You are fired.
>
> I want to break up with you.
>
> You are under arrest.
>
> How can I help you through this divorce, bankruptcy, foreclosure, lawsuit?
>
> Your account is overdrawn.

It's why they give you advice. They are communicating, "There is a better way." I am going to paraphrase what they are communicating, so that you will hear it. Here's what they really want to say:

Your way sucks!

Notice that I did not say that *you* suck; I said your *way* sucks (in the areas where you are effectively creating what you want, please disregard). The great news is that your extraordinary life does not require your way. In fact, it requires giving up your way. And since your way sucks, that should not be a problem.

Think about specific areas in your life that you are focused on how things should look versus being committed to the end result.

_____

_____

_____

_____

_____

RIDICULOUS LIST

Before we move on, let's cover the Ridiculous List. Most of you agree that it is ridiculous that someone has a goal to send cards and three weeks goes by without action because they didn't have the right stationery. Most of you agree that it is ridiculous that someone has a goal to read the Bible and three weeks goes by without action because there is a right way to read the Bible. Yet, you do this too! There are things you do, like Jessica, that are on your Ridiculous List. What are the reasons and excuses coming out of your mouth that are not true? Where are you letting small, minor details derail your goal? What are you spending time on that has nothing to do with your goal? What actions are you doing that sabotage your goal? What is coming out of your mouth that is absolutely *ridiculous*? Here are some examples for the Ridiculous List:

My goal is to weigh 135 pounds, yet I eat dessert every night.

I want to have a great relationship with my husband, yet blew up at him three times last night.

My goal is to write my book; however, I can't start until I know the title.

I am not able to start at the gym because my trainer is on vacation.

I find myself spending time on things like reading *People* or going to the movies. Both of these are not important to me AND have nothing to do with my goals.

Playing video games helps me clear my mind and focus.

It's amazing what can come out of your mouth when your limiting beliefs feel threatened. Some of those limiting beliefs are so strong they cause you to cling to the absurd as though it were rational.

Write down 10 items that belong on your Ridiculous List.

1. _____

2. _____

3. _____

4. _____

5. _____

6. _____

7. _____

8. _____

9. _____

10. _____

PROCRASTINATION AND AVOIDANCE

I once attended a seminar where the presenter gave an example of procrastination at its finest. He pretended to be a salesperson with the goal of making more networking calls. Throughout his presentation, he referred to an imaginary clock on the wall, thinking aloud for all of us to hear. Here's what he said:

At 8:00: "Oh, it's 8:00 a.m. I think I'll wait to call Mr. Smith until later. I mean, it's very early in the morning. I wouldn't want to wake him."

At 8:15: "Well, it's still early, so maybe I should wait a bit more."

At 8:30: "I'm going to check my e-mail first, and then I'll be sure to make the call."

At 8:45: "You know, most offices don't open until 9:00. I'd better wait until then."

At 9:00: "I'm sure he won't appreciate someone calling him the second he steps into his office."

At 9:15: "What if he got caught in traffic? Better give him a few more minutes."

This routine continued, and every 15 minutes the presenter talked himself out of making the call at every turn until 8:00 p.m. A large percentage of his justifications and rationalizations were logical *and familiar.*

Think about it: how often have *you* procrastinated? Put off making the phone call? Added another item to the "to do" list for tomorrow, because you failed to do the item today? Declared that the diet will begin "on Monday?" Told yourself you are too tired to meditate before going to bed? All of these are prime examples of procrastination, and if you allow this to become a habit, you won't ever get out of the gate. Forget about achieving your goal.

I was talking to a friend of mine about this book, and he mentioned his procrastination trigger words, "Beef Wellington." He reminded me of the time when he was in such resistance and avoidance that instead of working on his goals he decided that it was very important that he go home and learn how to make Beef Wellington. He made sure I remembered that Beef Wellington is the one with the puff pastry surrounding the meat. That definitely goes on the Ridiculous List.

When I asked John if he still used Beef Wellington as a trigger word for avoidance or procrastination, he said, "Well, I don't know if I necessarily use Beef Wellington as a trigger word, but I am familiar with my Beef Wellington avoidance pattern at this point. When I sense I am procrastinating, I usually just stop and say to myself, 'Focus, John,' usually aloud."

"I also surround myself with trinkets that are reminders of who I am and who I want to be. I have a Superman toy on my desk that my wife bought me, and an awesome handkerchief I bought in Japan that has dragons on it. While I don't necessarily identify with either dragons or Superman, they are reminders to me of strength and doing what is right.

"I will pick them up or move them to remind me to stay focused. I also keep a good fortune trinket I got at the Meiji Jingu Shinto Shrine, and my grandmother's Saint Anthony (saint of lost things) on my key chain. I don't attribute any luck to them but, again, they are physical reminders to stay on the correct path."

What can you do if you find yourself procrastinating? Awareness is the first step. Using triggers, as John mentioned, is a great way to stay aware. As soon as you catch yourself rationalizing, talking yourself out of taking action or find yourself avoiding, stop.

Recognize what you're doing. Immediately take forward action somewhere. It's even better if you can take action towards what you're avoiding. Don't wait another 15 minutes. Don't check your email, get a snack, or watch a TV show. Don't make Beef Wellington, unless your goal is to make Beef Wellington. You can take care of those things *later*.

In fact, if you have something else that you want to do, you can use it as a reward for yourself, rather than a way to put off doing what you really need to do. Consider the effect on your self-esteem when you have taken action. Realize the consequences for your self-esteem if you don't take action. Procrastination and avoidance are huge self-esteem chippers that you can stop in their tracks.

Where in your life is your single greatest area of procrastination?

What will you do TODAY to create movement in that area?

THE NOT-SO-GREAT STUFF

"Until the really 'great' stuff comes along, do the not-so-great stuff.
The not-so-great stuff always leads to the great stuff. Whereas doing nothing
pretty much leads to nowhere. And do it with passion."

- THE UNIVERSE -

All of the great stuff is created by the not-so-great stuff. If you are not willing to do the not-so-great stuff, you won't have very much great stuff. Consider working out five days a week for one hour at 5:00 a.m. over the course of 90 days. For some, that might be in the category called the not-so-great stuff.

Now, imagine on Day 91 being able to wear that bikini or fitting into the wedding dress; clearly, that's the great stuff. Maybe you are saving money in order to buy a house. During the year you save, you have to say no to vacations, new clothes, and doodads—the not-so-great stuff. The day you move into that house will be pretty great.

The not-so-great stuff always leads to the great stuff. *How much not-so-great stuff are you willing to do to get all the great stuff?* For most people, not very much. They would rather stay safe and comfortable and live by "If it feels good now, do it."

"Your future self has a message for you: take better care of your body, save more money, and do more not-so-great stuff. I need you."

- RENEE CERMAK -

How well (or not) you do the "small stuff" is a predictor of how you will do the "big stuff." If your boss is not able to count on you to keep two accounts moving forward, why would she give you 10? If you can't count on yourself to pay your bills on time, how will you count on yourself to build wealth?

If you can count on yourself to do the "not-so-great stuff" consistently and regularly, then you will be prepared to welcome the big rewards into your life. You will possess the self-esteem and habits to handle the greater responsibilities and rewards that go along with the "great stuff."

> "Don't be afraid to give your best to what seemingly are small jobs. Every time you conquer one, it makes you that much stronger. If you do the little jobs well, the big ones will tend to take care of themselves."
> - DALE CARNEGIE -

Also, keep in mind that in between the great moments are the not-so-great moments that prepare us for the next big moment. Meet Claire and Anne, two receptionists who work in the same office. Claire brings fun, passion, and solutions to everything she does. In addition, she can be counted on to not only complete her jobs well but also do more than expected. Anne, on the other hand, is average. She does just enough to get by. She arrives at work at the last minute and leaves the second she can clock out at the end of the day.

Despite their obvious differences, both women share a common goal as neither want to work as a receptionist forever. They have their eyes on higher-paying positions in the company that would entail greater responsibility and skills.

When a position opens, which person do you think the CEO will promote? It's a no-brainer, yet many people unintentionally live their lives like Anne. They fail to recognize that who they are speaks so loud, other people don't need to hear a word they are saying. They fail to see that by treating people, situations, and jobs with a bare minimum attitude, a condescending attitude, or even an average attitude, they are counting themselves out of the competition.

Some people fail to realize that the way they are being today (actions, behaviors, attitude) will affect future opportunities. As a result, they will fail to attract better opportunities that would lead to success, satisfaction, and joy. Keep in mind that you may not be in love with your current situation (job, relationship, etc.), but the challenge is for you to live a passionate life, no matter what. What if you embrace the *not-so-great?* Bringing passion to the not-so-great is a skill few people have, yet it's highly sought after, and it is simply created by a habit.

"A master's awareness of spiritual laws directs him or her to manifest major life changes by working with their thoughts, not by working harder.

Which isn't to say they don't sometimes work very long hours, because they do; they just don't think of it as work. Which also isn't to say they all have cool jobs that anyone would love, because they don't; they just see every task before them, no matter where they work, as a gift to unwrap.

Hmmmmm..."

- THE UNIVERSE -

TRANSITIONS

You will experience life events that may or may not be in your control. These are things that can seriously affect your self-esteem such as changing jobs, moving, divorce, health problems, losing a loved one, or retirement. Circumstances such as these can cause serious blows to your self-esteem. If you have areas in your life from which you derive a great deal of self-esteem, and those areas change, inevitably your self-esteem changes as well.

Some people never make the connection between their career and their self-esteem. So, when their career is gone, they are like a fish out of water. Some people never make the connection between their marriage and self-esteem. So, when their marriage is gone, they are dumbfounded by the loss. It is possible to anticipate and handle change and loss more effectively. The first step is becoming aware of the sources of your self-esteem. What are the major sources?

Some examples are career, making money, being a great parent, marriage, relationships, a successful business, your physical health, contributing to people, making a difference, and hobbies. What percentage of your self-esteem would you attribute to each? Do you derive 90% of your self-esteem from your career? Or do you have a variety of sources? If you get 90% from one source, then it is time to diversify. For the same reasons you diversify financially, it's too risky putting all of your eggs in one basket.

Remember that our self-esteem comes from the small daily, weekly, and monthly activities associated with these major sources. There are innumerable things you get to be proud of in a career, because it is not easy. There are countless things you get to be proud of in a marriage, because it is not easy. In case you haven't noticed, easy does not build self-esteem.

There is value in the struggle, there is value in doing things that are difficult, there is value in doing things that most other people don't do. What is the value? Increased self-esteem. Think of the butterfly struggling to get out of the cocoon. The struggle, the difficulty, is what gives the gift of wings and flight. If somebody does it for them, the wings don't build the strength they need, and the butterfly does not fly. *The struggle is real. Respect the struggle.*

If you know that something is on the horizon that may threaten your self-esteem, you can set up a plan to counteract the hits your self-esteem may take. For instance, if most of your department received pink slips and rumor has it there may be more cuts, you would be wise to anticipate how you will handle it if you lose your job. Just hoping it won't happen to you isn't enough, because if you haven't prepared adequately and the worst case scenario happens, you've wasted valuable time you could have used to shore up your resources and energy to be in a position to better handle whatever comes your way.

Imagine someone in the middle of a divorce. Let's say that this person derived 30% of their self-esteem from their marriage. They know that the source of 30% of their self-esteem is now gone. Not only that, but a new source for decreasing their self-esteem was just created: being divorced. What can they do?

They can find new sources to support their self-esteem, like taking that trip to Australia, starting a new exercise program, joining a club, contributing time to a nonprofit organization, or starting a new hobby. They can reinforce current sources of self-esteem like producing results at work, exercising more, spending more time with friends, and spending more quality time with their kids. The key is they can be proactive, set up a plan, and minimize the effects of the change.

In 2007, I really wanted a little time off—a retirement of sorts. I was burned out. At the time, I was facilitating personal growth seminars. I was aware that a good amount of my self-esteem came from making a lot of money, from being recognized in various ways, from making a significant difference in people's lives, and from working with a rare, high-level group of leaders.

I knew that if I chose to walk away from my career that the money, the recognition, and making a difference at that level was going to end. I knew that my self-esteem was going to take a huge hit. I had already recognized that my career contributed to my high level of self-esteem.

Even though I anticipated this transition, when the time came, leaving the organization hit my self-esteem harder than I expected. When a big source of my self-esteem ran dry—bringing in the money, feeling a sense of belonging, gaining the respect from colleagues—I wasn't quite sure how to handle it. I found myself second-guessing my decision. Since what you do here is what you do everywhere, I found myself full of doubt and indecision.

With the busyness and the urgency gone, I found myself deflated and lethargic at times. I was operating on a whole different frequency, a lower self-esteem frequency. Even vacations had lost their color, because they were now happening 12 times a year versus four. There was no urgency to make sure I had fun or went on adventures. If I didn't have fun on this one, there was always the next one.

Also, there was that voice in my head telling me that I hadn't done anything lately that was worthy of taking a vacation. I wasn't taking a vacation *from* anything. There is a subtle part of playing hard that requires working hard. I also found myself reading a lot of books for enjoyment and for avoidance. When there is less to do, it is easy to slow down the pace and have more time to find places to avoid.

So there were difficulties, especially in the beginning. Remember *The Dip?* However, day by day, things changed. I found new interests, new people, and new hobbies. I completed projects I had talked about for years. I adjusted to the slower pace, and even found there were benefits to it. I found self-esteem in places I didn't expect to find it.

I formed relationships with people that opened up new doors. I had time to collaborate about the slew of ideas jumbling around in my head. As a result of my short retirement, my husband and I partnered up and created a two-and-a-half-day wealth building seminar and a six-month wealth building program.

The genesis of this book happened during my retirement. If I had not retired and experienced the full extent of my self-esteem loss, I am not sure I would have realized the importance of self-esteem and the small stuff. I had to experience it firsthand. I had been spending 60 hours a week on work-related small stuff, I had tied up huge amounts of my time and resources in this single area of my life. I learned that I needed to add variety to my self-esteem sources.

What I find interesting about the retirement end-goal is that so many people spend their lives working really hard in order to get to the point where they can retire, only to find that when they have the freedom and time they wanted so much, they realize that what really gave them satisfaction and self-esteem was tied to their professional lives or raising children. For years, they called it the daily grind.

There is extensive fulfillment that comes from the daily grind. After all, you spend 80% of your life there. What is fulfilling is the great people you associate with, the leadership roles you play for people, the results you produce, the places where you belong, the difficulties you overcome, the experiences you have, and the man or woman you become through it all. Respect the grind. Without the grind, high self-esteem is not possible. Also, respect your parents. They went through at least two major self-esteem transitions with you: when you came and when you left.

As you think about your life and where it's headed at the moment, consider any possible transitions coming up. What is your game plan going to be if that change occurs? How will you be proactive versus reactive regarding your self-esteem?

Think about two possible transitions and actions you can take *now* so you can minimize the effects on your self-esteem.

Transition / Action #1:_____

Transition / Action #2:_____

Become aware of the sources of your self-esteem, and be willing to spend time diversifying. Protect your sources.

CHAPTER 9
YOUR PERSONAL SELF-ESTEEM PLAN:
USING THE CERMAK 1,000 BOX STRATEGY™

Now it is time to take everything you have learned so far and create your personal plan for increasing your self-esteem. The *Cermak 1,000 Box Strategy*™ will get you from where you are now to where you want to go. Think back to your self-esteem quiz from Chapter 1. The following strategy will help you bridge the gap between where you are now and where you declared you want to be.

If your self-esteem "score" is at a 70, and you aspire to an 80, you need to decide what actions you can take to move you toward your goal and improve your self-esteem. This strategy can be used to increase self-esteem, and it can be used to achieve goals. We will be looking at both.

In order to move from one level of self-esteem to the next, imagine there are 1,000 boxes in between your current number (70) and where you want to go (80). Your job is to fill in the 1,000 boxes with all of the small stuff that you have become aware of in this book. You have no idea which boxes are going to be the most important ones to move and improve you, so you have to do them all.

Think of it this way: if you are willing to throw 1,000 things against the wall, something is guaranteed to stick. If you are willing to fill in all 1,000 boxes, then the new picture of your self-esteem, your new level of self-esteem, will start to emerge.

The *Cermak 1,000 Box Strategy*™ is all about the small stuff—doing little things consistently. Every box relates to your self-esteem—

directly or indirectly. Some boxes might be filled with exercise, drinking water, and taking supplements. Others will include going to a seminar, taking classes or lessons, attending workshops and trainings, investing money, or spending time with a loved one.

Maybe your boxes will include joining new clubs, becoming part of a professional group, doing charity work, tithing, writing thank-you cards, engaging in a new hobby, or taking a vacation. As long as they relate to increasing your self-esteem, to you liking yourself more, any and all of these small things will fill in the boxes.

One thousand actions might sound overwhelming at first, but you're not doing all of them at once. Or you may wonder if each "box" will really make a difference in the end. Well, if we all had clear roadmaps of which of the 1,000 boxes we need to fill in order to be successful, life would be boring, and we would only complete the boxes that were necessary.

Life doesn't work that way. Most people, in hindsight, can appreciate all of their actions because each action will teach them what works— and what doesn't. The question is, are you willing to do *any* thing, *all* things (assuming legal, moral, and ethical) in your commitment to the goal in order to uncover which boxes were the most important?

What is *any* and *all* things? It's ALL things. Things that you might think are silly or unreasonable. Actions that you might not currently see the value in doing, actions that are inconvenient. Doing things that rub against your current beliefs, things that challenge you, that scare you. Doing things that other people suggest, even though you have already tried it. Doing things you don't want to do. Any and all things is NOT picking and choosing, it is not your way, it is not comfortable, it is not convenient.

The answer is only revealed to those people who are willing to do *all* of it. In your willingness to do *all* things, *any* thing, you will learn invaluable lessons about yourself.

> "Only in hindsight will the miracles become obvious, will you see you were guided, and will you find there was order all along. 'Otherwise,' as you once said, a long, long time ago, 'it would all be too easy...'
> We agreed."
>
> - THE UNIVERSE -

THE PICTURE UNDERNEATH

Remember the 50th birthday party for my husband? Something else really great happened as a result of that party: parts of this book were born. I received my first visual example of the *Cermak 1,000 Box Strategy*™ from two sources I would never have thought of: my sister, Erin, and my photographer. There was nothing futile about that party, including increasing my husband's self-esteem, even though my limiting belief, Sally (frugal/scarcity), thought the total amount of the bills was quite ridiculous at the time.

I had been teaching the small stuff and the 1,000 boxes for years. Because of that party, I had a way to visually back up the concept. My very creative sister, the event/party planner (her company is called Revolution), came up with an idea for my mother's 70th birthday that my husband liked and wanted to copy. We took a great photo of my husband with his Harley and sent it to my sister. She enlarged the picture and projected it onto a huge 8-foot by12-foot canvas.

Then, one of her employees spent 40 hours doing the not-so-great-stuff creating a pencil outline as well as the paint number that corresponded with each tiny section—like a gigantic paint by numbers painting with 10 different paint colors. Once the huge paint-by-numbers was finished, it was cut up into 96 pieces, each 1-foot square. When people arrived at the party, they received a square foot piece of canvas, a bib, and a paintbrush. Their job was to paint one square of the picture.

When each piece was dry, my sister attached them to an 8-foot by 12-foot plywood backdrop using Velcro and a numbering system. As the party went on, more of the picture was filled in. First 10%, then 33%, then 50%, then 64%. As the night continued, the picture came to life, one square at a time. Each square was seemingly unimportant, yet required for the whole. When my husband attached the last canvas, it was a masterpiece that everyone had participated in creating.

I love my sister's creativity. I met with my photographer a couple days later. He had taken photographs of the "mural" all night, through its developing stages, 0% all the way to 99%, and then the last piece. He then created a one-minute video that showed the progression of each box being filled in from a blank canvas to a completed picture consisting of 96 boxes. My life changed the moment he showed me that video and this book might not have happened without the clarity the video provided. He showed me a visual representation of what I had been teaching for years with the 1,000 boxes.

There is always a picture forming underneath your 1,000 boxes, one box at a time. Oftentimes, we are not able to see the picture. Therefore, we are not able to see our progress. It is easy to discount each of the small pieces as insignificant, not knowing they are all required. It is easy to fill in 10% of the boxes, not see the results, and give up. It is easy to fill in 50% of the canvas, not see the results you want, and give up.

It is even possible to fill in 97% of the picture and still not have a complete picture. In the case of my husband's mural, the last 3 squares to be placed were of my husband's face, so unless you were there, it was still not clear who the person in the picture was until the last 3%. So you give up, three feet from gold. Now imagine filling in 500 of your 1,000 boxes, doing 50% of the work, and still the picture is hazy; the results have not caught up with the effort. It is common to lose sight.

Every time you fill in a box, you are getting closer to the end-result picture, whether that is a picture of you with enormous self-esteem or a picture of you with an accomplished goal. Your end-result picture might be you walking down the aisle, speaking to 1,000 people, or a certain net worth. It is important to note that whether you are aware of it or not, small daily actions equal your future end result picture.

I remember calling two of my friends, Portia and Irene, one day and asking, "What are you guys doing today?" They answered, "We are very busy filling in boxes." They were working out, paying bills on time, handling incomplete projects, making phone calls for their money goal, getting pedicures, and taking actions to increase their credit score. Get together and fill in boxes. What a great idea!

There were at least 1,000 things that I needed to accomplish to finish, publish, and make my book available to the public. All the small stuff, though, came together to produce the goal of publishing the book. When I started this project, I didn't know which boxes would have the greatest impact. I had no idea that e-mails I saved from four years ago would end up being in my book.

Who knew that giving my husband a great 50th birthday would add to my book? I didn't know that experiences I had 10 or 20 years ago would be included. Who knew that my photographer would play a big role in giving me a valuable self-esteem tool? I started filling in boxes for writing a book long before I knew I was writing a book.

When you put a puzzle together, there are exciting parts: the people, the objects, and the action. Then there are some not-so-exciting parts: the background, the sky, the grass. The same is true with 1,000 boxes. Some boxes immediately appear very important or exciting, and then there are some boxes that are more on the fringe. You might not even know their value, yet they are required—vital for you to attain your goal.

For instance, every time I do a talk on self-esteem to a group of people, I am filling in one of the thousand boxes that move me to the end result of getting the book published. Even though the talk on self-esteem has nothing *directly* to do with the book being published, it has everything *indirectly* to do with it. The talk may be one of those border pieces, the boxes that I fill in and say, "Well, what does that have to do with the end result?" But every time I do the talk, I get clearer, and I have the opportunity to crystallize my ideas.

Filling in these seemingly futile boxes could open up new doors. There might be someone in the audience who might want to support my project. There might be a magazine publisher in the room who says, "Hey, we are doing a story on self-esteem and would like to promote your book." If I'm not willing to get out there and get clear on my subject, such an opportunity would not arise.

When I reach my goal and fill in all the boxes, I can look back and see exactly how I accomplished my goal. In hindsight, I might say, "Oh, it was really those 50 key boxes right there out of the thousand. Those 50 were the most important to getting my book published."

However, that's in retrospect. I had no idea that those were the 50 boxes that were going to make it happen when it was actually occurring. And yet, the other 950 were required to build a strong foundation. When it comes to the end result picture, you have to have faith. You have to believe that things are happening, that a picture is forming that you are not able to see, even when there is no evidence that the picture is taking shape.

NOTHING IS FUTILE

You must be willing to take many small actions, not knowing where the solutions are going to come from. Do the things that you know work, and do things even when you don't know if they will work. It's like throwing darts at a board; it isn't random—you're aiming for the bullseye.

Some of your actions will have immediate consequences that lead you to your goal and others will not make their importance known until 15 years down the line. Remember my friend Addy and her Great Date Game? Addy is now married to the man of her dreams. Is she married to someone she met during her game? No, but the game—being unreasonable, vulnerable, asking for help, and going on all of those great dates—absolutely prepared her and changed her into the woman that would attract her husband into her life.

Everything you do counts. Everything matters. *Everything speaks*. You don't know which actions are the most important (yet), which is why it's so important to fill in *all* the boxes!

"The real reason so many have trouble with the baby steps -- doing all they can, with what they've got, from where they are, no matter how humble or seemingly futile -- is because they haven't yet grasped that the baby steps trigger unseen forces that throw wide the floodgates of unstoppable momentum, infinite abundance, and eternal life.

Just some tiny steps."

- THE UNIVERSE -

To even have a shot, you have to start with those baby steps, that small stuff, that not-so-great-stuff. Sadly, most people aren't willing to do that because they're not able to see the end result, or they're not able to see how they're going to get there. It seems overwhelming and futile, and yet, *nothing* is futile.

    " Although I wanted to meet Mr. Right, my goal was to 'practice' dating, and so I set a goal to go on eight dates in 90 days. Duplicate dates with the same person would not count. This goal was about meeting new people.

    Date seven was fun. Joe and I actually ended up dating for a couple of months. I was okay with the way things were going, but I knew I wanted something real. My mentor challenged me to talk to Joe about what he wanted, just to make sure we were headed in the same direction. We were not. He had no interest in being in a relationship. We agreed that we were in different places in our life, and wished each other the best. But it hurt. It wasn't really about Joe. I was hurt because I could not understand why I wasn't meeting 'the one.' I was in the best shape of my life, cute, fun, smart.

    Why God? Why not me?

    I remember sitting in the park with my two dogs, crying. What was wrong with me? Why couldn't I find love?

    The crying cleared my mind. The next morning, I woke up with a new attitude. Joe was date number seven, and my goal was eight dates. A colleague of mine that knew about my dating goal had been pressuring me to go out with a man she knew. I had reservations. This woman had a negative attitude most of the time, she seemed angry at the world, but I wanted to get this dating goal over with. I told her to give him my number. He called three times before I called him back. After a five-minute conversation, he asked me out for that Friday night.

    Thirteen years later, I am so grateful for that evening in the park when I was crying with my dogs because that evening led me to my husband.

    It was the blind date that went right. I would never have expected that the negative colleague had the answer to my prayers. Thank God I finished that goal. One more date. Date eight was great! **"**

- Irene Montoya

There are so many great points in Irene's story. Stay committed to the completion of the goal, even if it is just to get it over with. When you are hit with failure, cry and move on. It would have been easy for Irene to give up after the seventh date, three feet from gold. She could have justified not going on another date for two years, and she would have missed out on something that the Universe had already set up.

The Universe already has a plan for you. The question is, will you be there to claim it? Irene had already done 7/8, or 87.5%, of the work, yet the end-result picture looked random; nothing tangible or clear. Her future husband was one degree of separation from her the entire time, and her solution came from an unlikely source. The solution often comes from an unlikely source, which is why you need to keep your mouth open, communicating to others what you want to create.

I want you to see a perfectly good example of using the *Cermak 1,000 Box Strategy*™ outside of the literal parameters. Let's say that you are brilliant, and you decide to set a goal of creating five new habits BEFORE you set a goal of completing a triathlon. Your five new habits are working out five days a week, drinking three liters of water daily, eating five meals per day, getting rid of fast food, and quitting smoking.

You are going to give yourself 90 days (12 weeks) to create the new habits. Your workouts will amount to 60 boxes. Your water intake will create 90 boxes. Your diet will amount to 90 boxes. Getting rid of fast food will lead to 90 boxes. Quitting smoking will amount to 90 boxes. The total is 420 boxes.

This is nowhere near the prescribed 1,000 boxes, yet look at where your life would be 90 days from now. *Significantly different.* Look at how prepared you would be for the next goal of a triathlon. You are free to use the *Cermak 1,000 Box Strategy*™ within the parameters or outside the parameters, just like life.

Greg is unemployed. He could just sit around all day, looking at the unemployment statistics. He could tell himself, "There are no jobs. It's not working. It's not going to happen, not for me." If he used the *Cermak 1,000 Box Strategy*™, however, he could change his thinking *and* behaviors.

Do you think that if Greg did 1,000 actions towards getting a job that he might end up with a job? He could polish up his resume, get online and see what jobs are out there, and send an email to his database.

But people are committed to their most familiar neural pathways. Even if he gets a bit optimistic, he may follow up those thoughts with limiting beliefs and doubts like, "But what's that really going to do? It may be more futile action."

Even though certain actions may not directly get Greg hired, just taking those initial actions that lead in the direction of the goal (getting a job) sets things in motion. Every time he goes on job websites, every time he mentions that he's looking for a job to friends and strangers, every time he submits a resume, he's filling in boxes.

Taking these steps brings about feelings of expectation and anticipation. These positive emotions will propel him forward and away from the feeling of being overwhelmed. He will be willing to fill in more boxes like going on practice interviews, shopping for a new interview outfit, or taking a class to improve his skills. When he does secure a job, he will look back and realize that even though certain boxes didn't directly get him the job, all of his combined actions *did* lead him to his successful end result.

"The few who look forward, while always knocking on new doors, no matter how futile it may seem or how insignificant their progress, will carry the many who just keep waiting for things to get better.

And the few will "suddenly" become overnight legends within their families, 'hoods, and countries, while having the most fun, with the most friends, at the most after-parties.

Win/Win, baby."

- THE UNIVERSE -

Nothing is futile. None of the boxes are futile. And the *Cermak 1,000 Box Strategy*™ can make it easier to fill in what are seemingly futile boxes. Sometimes you are just filling boxes for the sake of filling boxes. The more boxes you fill, no matter what the reason, the more opportunities that the Universe has to conspire on your behalf.

I believe that the Universe is constantly conspiring on your behalf. I believe that every night the Universe is setting up opportunities for you the next day: chance encounters, coincidences, and serendipitous moments.

The questions are: *Are you willing to fill in the boxes? Are you willing to do the work? Are you willing to increase your exposure to people, places, and experiences? Are you willing to expand your surface area to opportunities and solutions? Are you willing to be there—wherever "there" is?* "There" might be the networking event you were going to blow off. Or the blind date you almost turned down. Or starting a conversation on the subway instead of reading.

My friend Jason declares, "The deal of a lifetime happens every day." What if the opportunity of a lifetime happens daily, too? What if the relationship of a lifetime happens daily?

> "Being in the right place at the right time isn't something you can force. It just happens when you keep busy. Effortlessly. Imagine that."
>
> - THE UNIVERSE -

You might decide to interview 10 successful business owners about their successes and failures—filling 10 boxes, by the way. The man you interviewed at lunch #10 may end up being your $10 million investor five years from now. If you had not gone on lunch one through nine, the tenth would not have been possible. Where do you give up three feet from gold?

> "We don't start with baby steps for the distance we cover, we get started to even have a shot. Just telling friends on the phone your situation, being honest...balls start rolling and wheels start turning behind the curtains of time and space. There is a magic out there in life. We are not to worry about the how. WE are creators, we influence everywhere...from our own set of friends to others. If we have a dream and we're making baby steps and we have a commitment—things start happening. We summon resources we need from the unseen, beyond our physical senses, so that we will be predisposed to life's so-called coincidences. If we are thinking about it, moving with it, we will always be at the right place at the right time. People will be put on our path, an investor, a customer, a client, and those that don't fit the picture will be gently escorted to the side."
>
> - MIKE DOOLEY -

1,000 BOXES IN ACTION

Jeff sees the value in increasing the amount he likes himself, hence increasing his self-esteem. He recognizes that his self-esteem score of 73 is accurate, and that he has been consistently at that level for quite some time. He realizes that 73 represents the sometimes average, sometimes boring, sometimes stagnant parts of his life. Even though he seems successful to many, he is often unfulfilled.

There are things he wants to do that he is not doing. There are things he wants to learn that he is not learning. He wants to bring more of himself to the party to experience more adventure, love, fun, money, energy, and fulfillment. Most importantly, he wants to look in the mirror and really like who looks back. *Jeff wants to be his biggest fan.*

Jeff decides that he is going to focus on liking himself for 100 days and see what happens. He is going to make increasing his self-esteem his #1 priority. He is committed to raising his self-esteem score to 82. Using the *Cermak 1,000 Box Strategy™*, he is going to do 1,000 actions to like himself more in the next 100 days. His aim is 10 per day. His 1,000 boxes will include:

- Continuing to do the actions he already does to like himself.

- Doing the actions he already does more frequently or at a higher, more intense level.

- Doing new actions to like himself.

- Doing the actions he doesn't like about himself less often or not at all.

- Planned actions—spontaneous actions, big actions, small actions.

- Actions that are inconvenient, uncomfortable, new, repetitious, and hard.

- Actions that will be done only one time and actions that will be repeated daily or weekly, filling multiple boxes.

Here is what he came up with: There are 14 weeks in 100 days.
- Going out on 14 dates—1 date per week (5 of them blind dates) = 14 boxes
- Be on time to work 60 out of 70 days = 60 boxes

- Run a 5K = 1 box
- Call my mother and father 1x per week with no distractions = 14 boxes
- Take my parents to brunch 3x = 3 boxes
- Ask for a promotion (after 3 hours of preparation) = 4 boxes
- Work out 4x per week for a minimum of 45 min = 56 boxes
- Ride my motorcycle 20x, 5x for 1 hour or more = 20 boxes
- Buy 14 pair of new underwear = 1 box
- Buy new workout clothes = 1 box
- Buy new workout shoes = 1 box
- Plan and go visit a friend for a 3-day weekend = 4 boxes
- Introduce myself to 7 different neighbors = 7 boxes
- Write 5 "thank you for making a difference in my life" cards/letters = 5 boxes
- Wake up 1 hour earlier than my normal "rush" time 50x = 50 boxes
- Perform 1 random act of kindness every day = 100 boxes
- Take 7 salsa dancing lessons = 7 boxes
- Use a healthy, organic food delivery service for breakfast and dinner 3 days per week = 84 boxes
- Have my house cleaned every 2 weeks = 7 boxes
- Clean out my closet and donate my clothes = 2 boxes
- Go to church 10x = 10 boxes
- Put 10% of my income in my wealth building account weekly = 14 boxes
- Put 5% of my income in my tithing account weekly = 14 boxes
- Find 5 charities I am passionate about. Donate the 5% = 10 boxes
- Limit myself to 6 hours of television weekly = 14 boxes
- Spend 20 hours organizing home office = 20 boxes

- Spend 1 hour per week on wealth building education: online tutorials, reading books, taking classes. = 14 boxes
- Compliment 3 people per day 50 times = 50 boxes
- Drink 1 liter of water every day = 100 boxes
- Spend time with my niece – give her a ride home 1x per week = 14 boxes
- Floss my teeth 1x daily = 100 boxes
- Get my dental work handled = 5 boxes
- Send flowers to someone = 1 box

That totals 807 boxes, leaving Jeff 193 boxes for spontaneous, unplanned actions.

Jeff can hang signs to support his efforts. Signs that make him laugh, signs that cause him to take action, signs that cause him to get off autopilot. "What is 1 quick way I can like myself right now?" or "10 a Day!" or "How will I like myself today?" or "My self-esteem is my #1 priority; I am proving it daily."

My friend Heidi rated her self-esteem to be at a 60, and she wanted to improve upon this as she worked towards her first goal. She used the 1,000 boxes to reach her goal and increase her self-esteem at the same time. She worked through the S.M.A.R.T. goal attributes, and this was her finished written statement:

My goal is to weigh 140 pounds by the end of 90 days.

Heidi's compelling *why* was to be able to be more active and confident with her seven-year-old. She knew that he was forming his own food and exercise beliefs from her example. She completed her lists of what she was willing to do different, what she would stop doing, the prices she was willing to pay, and possible obstacles she could encounter.

Heidi told her husband, her best friend, and her mother about the goal, as well as all of her coworkers. All of them agreed to ask her at least once a week how she was doing. As she moved through her day, she continued to tell others about the goal and, by the end of the first five days, 24 new people knew she had a goal to lose weight.

She put signs on her refrigerator and in her car, and sticky notes on the mirror in the bathroom. She wore a necklace that reminded her of the goal every time she touched it.

After all that, she was ready to start filling in her boxes. She had already filled in 30 boxes just in preparing for the goal. She brainstormed a list of activities that would move her toward her ultimate goal. Even though she wasn't 100% sure which ones would pay off the most, she was committed to doing all the small stuff, knowing that eventually the cumulative effects of her efforts would benefit her. She began with actions that yielded positive results in the past:

Run for 30 minutes a day, three times/week

Take yoga classes twice a week (session = 90 minutes)

Eat breakfast daily

Replace soda with water

Take the stairs to the office instead of elevator

Park in furthest spot so I need to walk

Walk the dog one mile every day

Find a friend to join the gym with me

Eat a salad for lunch

Do 50 crunches/day

Meditate daily before work (15 minutes)

Cut down fast food consumption from current average of three times/week to once/week

Visit farmer's market weekly and buy seasonal produce

Switch over to organic fruits and vegetables

Substitute typical afternoon candy bar snack with granola bars

Switch from white bread to whole wheat and grains

Read nutrition books for more ideas

She used all of her tools to get to her goal. She not only accomplished her stated goal, but she also created considerable value in other areas of her life as a by-product of her 1,000 boxes exercise. When she looks back, she can clearly identify the 100 most effective boxes, the ones that moved her the farthest toward getting her goal.

The other 900 boxes raised her self-esteem by moving her forward in other areas of her life. Because she found a friend to join the gym with her, she strengthened that friendship. Because she meditated daily, she found greater peace and clarity in her life—seemingly unrelated to her goal of weight loss, yet incredibly valuable.

Sometimes the biggest value from achieving the goal doesn't

come from achieving the goal. Sometimes the biggest value comes from what new doors open—the opportunities that arise as a result of achieving the goal. Or the most value comes from the man or woman that you become as a result of achieving the goal.

When you are going straight at a goal, when you are in action, when you are filling in your 1,000 boxes, there are things that appear out of nowhere: golden nuggets, gems, gifts, chance meetings, coincidences, new doors, opportunities...miracles. While seemingly random at times, you see that each piece was necessary. You see how all of the pieces are intricately woven together to produce a brilliant end result.

In looking back, it may become clear that one of your past goals was just a stepping stone to something bigger. I mentioned I had been accepted to The Southwest College of Naturopathic Medicine in Arizona. Six months later, I moved to Tempe to pursue my medical career. I did not get a degree in medicine.

It turns out that attending medical school for two years was a stepping-stone for my current career of helping people be extraordinary. The Universe had to figure out a way to get me to Arizona. The key to all the gifts is staying in action and filling in boxes—so that the Universe can work its magic. Give the Universe something to work with. Give the Universe as much to work with as possible. Increase your exposure; expand your surface area.

"If you were to ask me I'd probably say that the number one cause of loneliness in time and space is not a lack of friends, but a lack of keeping busy. I'd even go so far as to say that nine out of 10 times the solution to every crisis, challenge, or problem—in relationships, careers, or otherwise—is to get busy. Because when you get busy, you allow me to slide whatever you most need—be it material, spiritual, or a new friend; answers, ideas, or comfort—right under your big ol' nose. Tallyho."

- THE UNIVERSE -

YOUR BOXES

Here are some ideas on how to personalize your boxes, whether for achieving goals or increasing your self-esteem or liking yourself more:

Do the actions that are on your "increase self-esteem" list.

Stop doing the things on your "decrease self-esteem" list.

What actions could you take to counter your limiting beliefs? How can you feed the "good" wolf?

What are actions you could take to give up being right?

What can you do to change the way you talk to yourself?

What do you want to see on your 24-hour/7-day video? Not want to see?

What boxes could you fill by creating new habits?

What activity could you start that you are interested in getting to the 100th time?

What actions will you take to improve your reputation with yourself and others?

What boxes could you fill by bringing more of yourself to the party?

Where, specifically, can you take the high road?

Where can you start tithing your time, treasure, and talent?

What actions could you take to take responsibility for past and current results?

What small stuff could you do to like yourself, respect yourself, and be proud of yourself?

What actions could you take to be selfish about your self-esteem?

Set goals.

What lessons, classes, workshops, and seminars will you take?

If $1 million were on the line, what would you do differently?

Exchange of value: how can you give your loved ones what they want? How can you go to the middle first?

What can you do to be unreasonable, abnormal, and uncommon? To separate yourself?

Where are you willing to give up your way? How?

How can you bring more fun and passion to the everyday?

What could you do to support a current or upcoming transition?

Start saying yes where you normally say no.

There will be overlap in your answers and strategy. We have looked at increasing self-esteem from at least 40 different angles. Remember the concept: *do them all, something will stick.* Be willing to do anything and everything, whether you know it will work or not, whether you have evidence or not.

If you are willing to do that day in and day out, then you will be successful. If you have done the work as you've gone along in this book, then it will be quite easy for you to personalize your plan. If you have not done the work, as my friend Kathy Quinlan-Perez would say, "Welcome to your life, people!" You have the option to change how you do things whenever you want. Choice can be changed moment by moment. Be urgent. Start immediately. Stay committed.

The Universe is conspiring on your behalf. *Always.*

CHAPTER TEN
TIME TO PLANT A TREE

Conclusions are hard to write. It is difficult, if not impossible, to conclude our conversation on this topic with a few more words of wisdom to send you on your journey to greater self-esteem. Although I have worked diligently for 19-plus years on my own self-esteem, I am still working, *every day*. I am still searching for answers, still fighting with my limiting beliefs, still establishing new habits, *still taking the steps that will make me my biggest fan*, and continuing to set goals that sometimes seem simply too big for me.

I like myself a lot more than I did 19 years ago, and yet there is still room for me to like myself even more. The lesson I've learned is that building self-esteem is a marathon, not a sprint. I can summarize for you my own journey, invite you to explore your own life, and challenge you to advance your own self-esteem. I can tell you how liking yourself is the greatest gift you could ever possibly give yourself. Yet, you must find out for yourself.

I don't know you, and yet I know that reading this book meant taking a chance on yourself. Taking a chance on a future you have only dreamed about. I admire and respect people who are willing to learn, willing to explore the edges, willing to do something different.

This can be a painful experience. It can also be exhilarating.

"The truth will set you free, but first it will piss you off."

- GLORIA STEINEM -

Self-esteem alone can help you create the amazing life you dream about, the extraordinary life that you deserve. I have given you everything I know of to help you along on your journey. I hope you can see in my examples, and in your own life, how and why self-esteem must be your #1 priority in life. For the sake of your own success, and for the sake of the world we live in, you must create ways to like yourself, to love yourself.

Remember, the struggle is real. Embrace the struggle. The daily grind has value. Respect the grind. Tension seeks resolution. Value the tension.

"Put yourself in a perpetual state of preparation and discomfort. If you have 6 hours to cut down the tree, spend 4 hours sharpening the ax."

- LES BROWN -

If you have 365 days to get a goal done, spend 243 days on building the self-esteem you'll need to get it done.

I encourage you to look for self-esteem opportunities for yourself and your family. Seek them out. Make a game of it. Do not wait for them to find you, and soon you'll see that self-esteem opportunities are everywhere.

You receive an e-mail from your cousin, asking you to donate money to her Breast Cancer Walk. She tells you that she wanted to do the walk for the past three years, but she was scared to raise the money. You think, "This looks like a self-esteem opportunity."

Your child ruined your favorite sweater accidently. You are on the verge of going to "Schmuckville." You think, "This could be a self-esteem opportunity."

You see the woman boarding the plane in front of you struggling with her child, car seat, and baggage. You think, "This looks like a self-esteem opportunity."

You find a wallet filled with money when you are playing in the park with your child. Your child says, "This looks like a self-esteem opportunity."

You are asleep in the car on a family road trip. You wake up because you feel your husband pulling off the road and stopping. You ask, "Why are we stopping?" and at the same time your husband and your children yell out, "It's a self-esteem opportunity!" Then you notice the elderly man and his flat tire.

The rest of your life...it looks like a self-esteem opportunity!

"The Chinese say, 'The best time to plant a tree was always 20 years ago. The second best time is always today.' Funny how planting trees and taking action on the life of your dreams are the same that way."

- THE UNIVERSE -

FILL IN YOUR 1,000 BOXES ONLINE

I have created an interactive website to help you continue this work. A place where you can set goals and increase the amount you like yourself by using the *Cermak 1000 Box Strategy* ™.

The website is a creative and productive space to help you build your personal, specific, and strategic 1000 box self-esteem plan. It offers you over 1,000 options, in a variety of categories, to fill your boxes. Categories like Health & Wellness, Love & Romance, Wealth & Finance, and Fun & Adventure.

You can concentrate in one category, or you can pick and choose.

You will be able to choose the duration of your program (30, 60, 90 days, etc.) and the number of boxes that you will complete (500, 750, 1000, etc.). You can also upload a picture of your vision board, symbolizing the end result, which will be revealed one box at a time as you take action. I encourage you to continue this work there. Your next steps are vital. It is easy to fully appreciate and value a book and still take no action. Please take action!

You can connect to the website at: 1000BoxStrategy.com

EPILOGUE

I am confident that your self-esteem has already risen since you started this book, and that you have begun filling in many of your 1,000 boxes. My wish is that you are starting to put your self-esteem first in your life, just as I am and have done. I am going to leave you with a story that is worth revisiting regularly on your personal growth journey.

Meet Helen and Rachel. Five years ago, Helen and Rachel had a budding friendship. Rachel was dating a jerk. The jerk did not like Helen or Helen's friends. He knew that Helen had new doors to open for Rachel. He convinced Rachel that she should cut off all contact, and so she did. When she did, she was not so nice about it. She accused Helen of things, and she even did something against one of her core values: integrity.

Years went by, and Rachel matured. She dumped the jerk and married a prince. She created a successful business and had her dream baby. All the while, during those five years, she would think about Helen. She would replay the video of her actions, her words, and her lack of integrity. She would be forced to look at how she chose to handle the situation. Odd things would trigger her to remember. When the subject of integrity came up, she always remembered what she had done, and every time it would chip away at her self-esteem. Every time this happened, she would think about picking up the phone and making a call that would make it all right.

However, the parts of her that wanted to stay safe and comfortable won. She never made the call. That caused her to chip at her self-esteem more.

One day, five years after the incident, Rachel saw Helen. She mustered up all of the courage she had and marched right up to Helen and said, "I want to apologize for my actions and behaviors five years ago. There is no excuse for what I did. I have thought about calling you hundreds of times over the years to apologize, and I never took the risk."

Helen replied, "Don't you worry about it. It is so great to see you." And she meant it.

There are many variations to this story. "Helen" and "Rachel" could be significant others, friends, coworkers, business partners, or family members. Sometimes you are Helen, showing forgiveness and high self-esteem; sometimes you are Rachel, letting your deeply-ingrained beliefs and habits keep you from doing what you know is right. Most of us have experienced both roles; it's a common story.

Building self-esteem is not about getting it right the first time, and it is not about being perfect from here on out. Progress is better than perfection. Maybe prior to this self-esteem knowledge, you behaved like Rachel, and it took you five years to pick up the phone and make it right. Maybe now that you know, the next time it only takes you one year to make it right. The next time, six months. Then one month. Finally, one day you realize how precious your self-esteem is and that there is NOTHING worth chipping at your self-esteem, and you pick up the phone immediately, not even letting 15 minutes go by.

Maybe right now you act like Helen 40% of the time and Rachel 60%. Can you imagine a time in your life when you will be operating from integrity, compassion, and outward focus 99.9% of the time with incredible self-esteem?

Do you see the different versions of yourself getting better over time? It might take some time and some work, but it is time to show yourself and the world the BEST version of you.

The Man in The Glass

When you get what you want in your struggle for self
And the world makes you king for a day,
Just go to a mirror and look at yourself,
And see what THAT man has to say.

For it isn't your father or mother or wife
Whose judgment upon you must pass,
The fellow whose verdict counts most in your life
Is the one staring back from the glass.

Some people may think you a straight-shootin' chum
And call you a wonderful guy,
But the man in the glass says you're only a bum
If you can't look him straight in the eye.

He's the fellow to please, never mind all the rest
For he's with you clear up to the end,
And you've passed your most dangerous, difficult test
If the man in the glass is your friend.

You may fool the whole world down the pathway of years
And get pats on the back as you pass,
But your final reward will be heartaches and tears
If you've cheated the man in the glass.

Author Unknown

ACKNOWLEDGMENTS

Thank you to all of my friends and mentors from PSI Seminars... Jane Wilhite, Shirley Hunt, Bob Proctor, Kathy Quinlan Perez, Rob Rohe, Gary Perez, Tim O'Kelley, Courtland Warren, Bruce Conching, Carson Johns, Dan Gibbons, and Teresa Corbitt. I have learned so much from all of you.

I am grateful to my husband, Fred Auzenne, for making sure everything stays interesting. You are my greatest example of willing to be a beginner, committed to being a learner, and doing the opposite of most people. Thank you to my daughter, Penelope, for reminding me that every day is a new day to be adventurous, excited, and grateful. Thank you to my family: Carol, Jim, John, Dawn, Erin, Gail, Steve, Robin, Jamie, Beth, and the rest of my extensive, fun, fabulous family in Maryland and beyond. I am proud to be a Cermak.

I would like to acknowledge the following people for helping me along the way: Amy Hillman, Elizabeth Gilray Moreno, Jessica Blesoff Carter, Ingrid Rohrmoser Whitmore, Lynee Berner, Jane Thill, Jesse Armstrong, Kristin Roehmer, Helen Hain, Catherine Biggers, Mark and Tina Shearon, Bridget Clark, Portia Abrenica, Rebecca and Ron Finken, Brett Williams, Tracy King, Matt Baumann, Addy Logsdon, Nicole Thompson, Jenn Culver, Kristen Melton, Angela Cook, Michelle Kibel, Scott Havice, Myles Schrag, Jennifer Kahtz, and Marc Gleeman. And to Kathy Quinlan, my foxhole buddy, thank you.

I would like to acknowledge everyone who contributed personal stories: Bridget Clark, Jenny McCall, Matt Moses, Erin Cermak,

Nicole Thompson, Jessica Morel, Addy Logsdon, Renae Rochon, Kelli Allan, Angela Cook, Anton Visser, and Irene Montoya.

And to myself...woo-hoo! Nice job! Way to go! Thank you for being committed to the end result, even if it took five years. Done is better than perfect!

ABOUT THE AUTHOR

 Renee Cermak, self-esteem expert and author, is on a mission to help others lead an extraordinary life by making their self-esteem—how much they like themselves—their #1 priority. She accomplishes this through her dynamic, no-bullshit coaching methods, serving as a catalyst for lifelong change in people's lives. She coaches people to live a better life, their best life!

For the last nineteen years, she has been focused on personal growth. She is committed to leading by example through coaching, speaking, facilitating, writing, and, most importantly, actually doing the hard work to improve her own self-esteem and results. Renee believes self-esteem is not derived from the big moments in life but rather from everyday moments, the daily grind—the things we do or don't do, the things we say or don't say. Though they are subtle and easy to discount, these moments add up to produce significant results, both good and bad.

She serves as a consultant and facilitator for a leading authority and pioneer in human potential training. On a daily basis, she works with leaders who are committed to extraordinary lives and are willing to do the work to get there. Let Renee's book, *How to Be Your Biggest Fan*, be the catalyst for a lifelong change in your own life.

Renee and her husband, Fred, are entrepreneurs, business owners, investors, and philanthropists. They are also passionate about teaching seminars on the value of wealth building and the power of giving. They live in Scottsdale, Arizona, with their daughter.

REFERENCES

- Chandler, Steve. *Reinventing Yourself: How to Become the Person You've Always Wanted to Be*: Career Press, 2005

- Fritz, Robert. *The Path of Least Resistance: Learning to Become the Creative Force in Your Own Life*, New York, NY: Fawcett Books, 1989

- Hansen, Mark Victor. *The Miracle of Tithing*: 1996

- Mike, Dr. John. *Brilliant Babies, Powerful Adults: Awaken the Genius Within*, Satori Press, 1997

- https://faculty.washington.edu/chudler/plast.html

- 1. Gopnic, A., Meltzoff, A., Kuhl, P. (1999). *The Scientist in the Crib: What Early Learning Tells Us About the Mind*, New York, NY: HarperCollins Publishers.

- http://www.whatisneuroplasticity.com/pathways.php

REVOLUTION

EVENT DESIGN AND PRODUCTION

WWW.EVENTREVOLUTION.COM | 410.539.7236

2000 WASHINGTON BLVD SUITE 2010B BALTIMORE, MD

Erin Cermak: etc@eventrevolution.com